Y0-DIH-329

LYRICISM IN THE POETRY OF T. S. ELIOT

Kennikat Press
National University Publications
Literary Criticism Series

ANN P. BRADY

LYRICISM
in the
POETRY OF T. S. ELIOT

National University Publications
KENNIKAT PRESS // 1978
Port Washington, N. Y. // London

Manufactured in the United States of America

Published by
Kennikat Press Corp.
Port Washington, N. Y. / London

Library of Congress Cataloging in Publication Data

Brady, Ann Patrick.
Lyricism in the poetry of T. S. Eliot.

(National university publications) (Literary criticism series)
Bibliography: p.
Includes index.
1. Eliot, Thomas Stearns, 1888–1965–Criticism and interpretation. 2. Lyric poetry–History and criticism.
I. Title.
PS 3509.L43Z6443 821'.9'12 77-788
ISBN 0-8046-9183-5

CONTENTS

LYRICISM IN THE POETRY OF T. S. ELIOT

ABBREVIATIONS

PP *On Poetry and Poets*

SE *Selected Essays*

UP *The Use of Poetry and the Use of Criticism*

CHAPTER ONE

THE THEORY OF THE LYRIC:
ELIOT AND THE TRADITION

T. S. Eliot's value as poet and critic has been discussed in many fine studies since the master-handlings by F. O. Matthiessen in 1935[1] and Helen Gardner in 1949.[2] But one important aspect of both Eliot's theory and practice has been paid only passing and nonspecific notice; namely, his concept and execution of lyric verse per se. In reading any of the works of explication on *Four Quartets,* for example, one finds a common pattern regarding the fourth-section lyrics of these poems. These self-contained, short sections are commonly passed over in summary explication, while only a nod is given to their technique before the critic moves on to expound the crucial fifth sections which culminate each separate quartet. In view of the importance Eliot puts on transitional prosaic passages,[3] the self-containment of the lyric fourth sections is both striking and significant. Closer reading of these sections will reveal that each is the core of the entire quartet of which it constitutes the smallest single part. Eliot once wrote that "poetry is poetry, and the surface is as marvelous as the core."[4] In the case of *Four Quartets* one might contend that the core is as marvellous as the surface, and that a longer look needs to be given the core passages in the fourth sections. The need to evaluate these lyrics properly is part of the larger urge to keep reevaluating the quartets themselves, which Eliot considered his best work but which many readers consider a falling-off from the poetry of *The Waste Land.* This manifest urge for reevaluation is evidenced in the many works of explication on Eliot's poems, and it is a legitimate one. Aristotle said that the end of a work of art is contemplation. Eliot agrees with this principle when he writes: "Our impulse to interpret a work of art . . . is exactly as imperative and fundamental as our impulse to interpret the universe by metaphysics."[5] With *Four Quartets* a reader confronts both impulses inseparably bound because Eliot is interpreting the world and time and life itself in these contemplative pieces.

The object of this study is to investigate T. S. Eliot in regard to that very elusive and omnipresent genre of literary history, the lyric. Eliot is a very good practitioner in lyric poetry and continually comments on the art of the lyric in his critical works. An examination of his finest lyric practice in the light of his theory on the subject will further illuminate the unity of Eliot as poet and critic, and quite possibly shed more light on the *Four Quartets,* whose core passages are self-contained lyrics of a very high caliber, each one emanating from a time-honored tradition yet each remarkably original. Truly these lyrics embody the double quality Eliot praises in "Tradition and the Individual Talent" in 1919: ". . . we shall often find that not only the best, but the most individual parts of [a poet's] work may be those in which the dead poets, his ancestors, assert their immortality most vigorously."[6] Nowhere is Eliot more original than in these lyrics, and nowhere are the voices of the lyric tradition more clearly heard in his work.

When speaking of the lyric, one is faced with the problem of definition—a task which, practically speaking, can be both interminable and fruitless unless one takes note of the basic assumptions of the lyric tradition. Critics and literary historians have defined the lyric variously, but tradition runs roughshod over any definition too categorical or too contrived. The Chicago Critics come to mind immediately. Elder Olson's ponderous manipulation of the *Poetics* to include the lyric as a legitimate Aristotelian category is a case in point.[7] For all its ingeniousness it is less useful for understanding the lyric problem than his simple and straightforward discussion of the genre in the introduction to his anthology *American Lyric Poems.*[8] In the one case Olson constructs an abstract categorization; in the other he follows the tradition and simply describes what has always been. If one desires to communicate ideas on the lyric nature of a single poem or a number of poems, he must have a common currency of basic assumptions with other readers of poetry. In discussing any literary genre he can work only within the categories honored by tradition and put up with all the indefiniteness tradition seems to sustain regarding the demarcations of those categories. If, for example, a critic feels a strong compulsion to argue the case for Samuel Johnson's *Rasselas* as a novel, he can do so only in terms of the traditional assumptions about what constitutes a novel as such. With these assumptions as a negotiable base, he can proceed to show how *Rasselas* fits the qualifications traditionally accepted as endemic to the genre of the novel. He might need superhuman luck to succeed, but his method would at least be sound. If James Joyce's *Ulysses* is to be classed as an epic, it must prove itself a heroic poem and demonstrate its kinship with the poems traditionally accepted within the epic genre. Homer, Virgil, Dante, and Milton would constitute the norm by which the Joyce work would have to be judged. The same procedure applies to lyric poems.

According to tradition the term "lyric" has been applied to poems whose musical roots are apparent. The song, the sung lyric, poses no problems of identification, but when poems move away from a musical encasement, definitions break down and different opinions ensue regarding their classifications. These differences, however, are all grounded upon one universally agreed to principle: the affinity of the poem to music. The questions, the uncertainties, and the disagreements actually move from a firm base and depend on how far one is willing to stretch the categories of musical affinity. To what extent, for example, does one expect to find musical regularity in a lyric poem? To what extent does one consider complication of sound structure as a substitute for music proper? It is worth noting also that within this principle of musical adherence lies the norm for all value judgments of lyric verse: the norm of fitness. Just as a song is judged upon whether or not the music and words are suited to each other, so too the unsung lyric is judged on how well the various sound structures fit the meaning. The rhythm of Poe's "The Bells" could hardly be used to convey the message of Tennyson's "Sweet and Low." The stanzaic arrangement of Keats's "Ode to a Nightingale" would not do well for Donne's "The Sunne Rising."

It is important to take stock of those qualifications related to music which traditionally comprise the ingredients of lyric verse. The lyric is based in music, but the music of the song, not the symphony. As song the lyric tends to be short—a singable entity rendered more suitably by a single voice than by a chorus. As song, moreover, the lyric is inherently dramatic: every song has a singer and a chosen hearer. Because of its dramatic structure the address itself, the song proper, can be construed as a personal expression, not of the poet himself but of the singer of the song, the persona, the voice.[9] When considered in this way, the traditional qualities associated with the lyric are not so arbitrary. Brevity, dramatic structure, personal expression, regularity of meter are all qualities inherent in the lyric's foundation in the music of song.

One elusive point concerns the matter of sound itself. The words of a sung lyric can be simple and relatively unmoving in themselves, depending on the musical setting for their emotional power. Take, for example, the profoundly moving Negro spiritual "Sometimes I Feel like a Motherless Child." The words comprise one simple sentence: "Sometimes I feel like a motherless child a long way from home." But the pattern of phrase repetition, the significant alternation of melodic line, and the long sustaining of single words give an emotional quality impossible to attain by human speech unaided. This musical component is replaced in the spoken lyric by alternative sound-structures, sometimes of great complexity. The question is how much complexity can a poem take before the sound-structure moves away from its base in song? Once again the assumption is firm while the application may be ambivalent.

Considering the lyric in this way, one sees that the basic assumptions of music are behind all the arguments of categorization. Whereas readers disagree whether to classify Browning's "My Last Duchess" as a lyric, few would question the position of "Abt Volger" in that category. Both poems are dramatic monologues, but does the Duke of Ferrara speak in sufficiently regular verse to warrant the poem's affinity to a musical base in song? Does he speak in measures too near to the stage itself, closer to the speech of drama proper? The stanzaic pattern of "Abt Vogler" gives the poem a musical regularity more in keeping with the lyric tradition. When readers disagree about the lyric nature of such poems as Milton's "On the Morning of Christ's Nativity," their problem lies in the length and in the nature of the rhetorical structure. Is the ode too public in statement, less simply dramatic than rhetorical, less the utterance of a single voice and more the statement of a chorus? The musical setting for Milton's "Nativity Ode" bears out the validity of some of these doubts. Surely Cyril Bradley Rootham's composition for soloists, chorus, and orchestra is symphonic rather than lyrical.[10] Questions arise concerning the length of Spenser's "Epithalamion." They are answered by a reference to the divisions of the poem into smaller sections of musical regularity punctuated by a refrain. Yet one look at R. Vaughan Williams's 66-page cantata tends to throw one back upon the questions once again.[11] These matters will always be the focal points of critical disagreement on the lyric nature of particular poems. But the questions are based on assumptions which remain unquestioned and are universally agreed to in principle within the entire tradition of lyric verse.

Literary theory, therefore, can be said to exhibit a firm and constant base of insistence on musical affinity in defining the lyric genre. At the same time that base has been continually stretched to include the utmost fringe of musicality in regard to length, sound-structure, and dramatic quality. This kind of ambivalence inheres in the study of the lyric and can be very frustrating if one's energy and attention are diverted toward pinning down the undefinable into air-tight categories. The only sane approach is to perceive and accept the very steady base which is the consensus of tradition, and then adjust one's perception to particular deviations as they occur.

One finds such a procedure in T. S. Eliot's handling of the lyric throughout his body of criticism. Eliot treats the lyric in various places throughout the essays, and the reader may at first be put off by the difficulty in discerning any systematic handling of the problem of definition. For in an attempt to find a systematic treatment of the lyric or anything else in

T. S. Eliot's body of criticism, one is confronted immediately with the problem of terminology. At times Eliot defines his terms, occasionally even coining them when precision and clarity call for such a step. But when definitions seem undesirable because certain words have never been clarified in the history of their use, Eliot explicitly plies his terms in all their ambivalence, making no attempt at pinpointing, no apology for apparent imprecision. One such explicit justification comes at the end of his essay on Kipling, throughout which he has constantly employed the terms "verse" and "poetry" in contradistinction, yet with no attempt at definition: "I make no apology for having used the terms 'verse' and 'poetry' in a loose way. . . . Where terminology is loose, where we have not the vocabulary for distinctions which we feel, our only precision is found in being aware of the imperfection of our tools, and of the different senses in which we are using the same words."[12]

As far as the lyric is concerned, Eliot states outright that it is undefinable:

> The term "lyric" itself is unsatisfactory. We think first of verse intended to be sung. . . . But we apply it also to poetry that was never intended for a musical setting, or which we dissociated from its music. . . . The very definition of "lyric," in the *Oxford Dictionary,* indicates that the word cannot be satisfactorily defined:
>
> > Lyric: Now the name for short poems, usually divided into stanzas or strophes, and directly expressing the poet's own thoughts and sentiments.
>
> How short does a poem have to be, to be called a "lyric"? The emphasis on brevity, and the suggestion of division into stanzas, seems residual from the association of the voice with music. But there is no necessary relation between brevity and the expression of the poet's own thoughts and feelings. (*PP,* p. 105)

To illustrate his point Eliot cites "Hark! hark! the lark" and "Come unto these yellow sands," which are universally considered lyrics, but which in no determinable way express directly the poet's thoughts and feelings. On the other hand there are many long poems—Eliot cites *London, The Vanity of Human Wishes,* and *The Deserted Village*—which appear to express the poets' own thoughts and sentiments, but are nowhere considered to be lyrics.[13]

These remarks in "The Three Voices of Poetry" comprise Eliot's longest statement on the definition of lyric. Made rather late (1953), this "raid on the inarticulate with shabby equipment" justifies or explains his continual avoidance of definition in terms, though he deals frequently with lyric verse in his criticism. In 1936 he praises the lyrics of *The Princess* as among the greatest of their kind.[14] What that kind is he does not explain. In 1932 he lauds the lyric as the second great accomplishment of the Elizabethan age, but here he refers specifically to the sung lyric of Campion and Shakespeare, which owes its beauty not to rime or perfection of verse form, but to musical form (*UP,* p. 31). Twelve years later Eliot again stresses the integral function of the musical form to Campion's lyrics. They need to be sung, and the listener must have an appreciation of Tudor music to do this.[15] On the other hand he continually refers to the works of Donne, Marvell, Vaughan, and Herbert as lyrics; he follows the custom of applying the term "lyric" to the works of the Romantic poets. He speaks of Goethe as "a great lyric poet."[16] Eliot even goes so far as to bring the ideas of "thoughts and sentiments" into his own perception of the term. In his 1940 essay on Yeats, Eliot says that he does not consider his own work as lyric in the sense that Yeats's is lyric: ". . . and by this I mean rather a certain kind of selection of emotion rather than particular metrical forms."[17]

For all of Eliot's dissatisfaction with the *OED* definition of lyric, he nevertheless employs the word with the same traditional applications of metrics and tone indicated there. When he speaks of lyric, he is always concerned with measured verse and with a transmutation of some kind of thought and emotion into a communicable medium of language. In spite of his annoyance with the fact that "lyric" has no definition in the history of literature, he uses it with all the ambiguity of its cumulative associations, applying it to those poems and poets to whom it has been traditionally applied.[18] As he notes in the passage from the Kipling essay quoted above: "Our only precision is found in being aware of the imperfection of our tools, and of the different sense in which we are using the same words." The problem of definition of lyric poetry cannot be solved categorically by a study of Eliot's critical writings, precisely because Eliot plies the term with a healthy acceptance of the ambivalence inherent in a long and untidy tradition.

This problem granted, Eliot nevertheless has something which approximates a theory on lyric poetry. This theory is normative rather than definitive. Given that there is no precisely definable entity involved in the classification of "lyric," Eliot nevertheless has much to say on what qualities that poetry should have. It is a theory determined by cataloguing his repetitions. Eliot continually stresses the same points, and it is difficult to see any of these as not classifiable under the general concept of fitness: the coinciding of techniques and meanings in the making of a poem. For this reason he considers the function of criticism to be integral to that of composition: "The critical activity finds its highest, its true fulfillment in a kind of union with creation in the labor of the artist."[19] It might be well, then, to note what Eliot considers to be the proper points to observe in a critical evaluation of a poem, for these are what he considers to be the proper constituents of the poem itself. In the introduction to *The Use of Poetry* he wishes "we might dispose more attention to correctness of expression, to the clarity or obscurity, to the grammatical precision or inaccuracy, to the choice of words whether just or improper, exalted or vulgar, of our verse" (pp. 15–16). Elsewhere he notes that two of the deficiencies of Samuel Johnson's criticism are his overlooking the grammatical faults in Thomas Hobbes and his not taking notice of the musical quality of Shakespeare's verse. He poses a catalogue of what poetic evaluation should focus on:

> The question whether a poem is well or ill written, whether it could be improved, whether the cadences are musical, whether the choice of words is fastidious and literate, whether the imagery is happily found and properly distributed, whether the syntax is correct and whether the violations of normal construction are justified.

Eliot considers these the most valuable critical focal points because they are precisely the most important items that go into the making of a poem. They are the factors the poet should be conscious of in the art of making.[20]

These are the very things Eliot reiterates in his essays. Always these items are judged on their fitness to the whole structure and to the meaning. Considering that the nature of Eliot's criticism is scattered and occasional, one is impressed by his consistency on certain points of style, structure, fitness to a total pattern. Eliot himself has said that these repetitions are significant: "An unconscious repetition may be evidence of one's firmest convictions, or one's most abiding interests."[21] It is on these points, continually stressed by Eliot in his treatment of poetry, that the following investigations of his own lyric practice will be made.

CHAPTER TWO

ELIOT'S DEVELOPMENT AS A LYRIC POET

As a lyric practitioner T. S. Eliot developed to a considerable degree toward clarity. His early lyrics, for example, do not exemplify so well or so consistently those qualities peculiarly necessary for lyric verse which characterize the later works. The obscure characters and the difficult syntax endemic to Eliot through the 1920s are inimical to the sort of clarity demanded of lyric verse. The later poetry, however, presents its own problems to readers who are insensible to the religious nature of its content. The problem of communication, whether due to obscurity in manner and content or to reader incapacity, remains a factor throughout Eliot's poetic career and may not be skirted. After all, Eliot himself has said, "What a poem means is as much what it means to others as what it means to the author" (*UP,* p. 122). In a search for meaning perhaps too much critical effort has been expended on ferreting out autobiographical data and psychological information about the author and not enough on the poem itself. In *The Use of Poetry* Eliot complained about this trait in Matthew Arnold's critical works (p. 108); and in an essay for the *Nation and Athenaeum* dealing with "The Problems of the Shakespeare Sonnets," he cautions strongly against the method of autobiographical interpretation, while praising a critic's reliance on exact texts rather than upon personal enthusiasm for the poet's supposed experience: "A fine poem which appears to be the record of a particular experience may be the work of a man who has never had that experience; or a poem which *is* the record of a particular experience may bear no trace of that or of any experience. . . . I do not say that poetry is not 'autobiographical': but this autobiography is written by a foreign man in a foreign tongue, which can never be translated."[1] As far back as "Tradition and the Individual Talent" (1919), Eliot was concerned with this problem in criticism: "To divert interest from the poet to the poetry is a laudable aim: for it would conduce to a juster estimation of actual poetry, good and bad" (*SE,* p. 11).

These efforts along autobiographical lines in literary criticism often fail to shed light on what the poem is there to communicate.

> If poetry is a form of "communication," yet that which is to be communicated is the poem itself, and only incidentally the experience and the thought which have gone into it. The poem's existence is somewhere between the writer and the reader; it has a reality which is not simply the reality of what the writer is trying to "express," or of his experience of writing it, or of the experience of the reader or of the writer as reader. Consequently the problem of what a poem "means" is a good deal more difficult than it at first appears. (*UP,* p. 21)

The problem of communication is one to which Eliot addressed himself throughout his critical career. He may state in *The Use of Poetry* that " 'communication' will not explain poetry," but he goes on to note that poetry could not exist without "communication taking place" (p. 131). And twenty years after the preceding statement, he remarks: "If the poem were exclusively for the author, it would be a poem in a private and unknown language; and the poem which was a poem only for the author would not be a poem at all."[2] Though Eliot insists that a poem needs to communicate something, he insists likewise that its content might be more than that intended by the author. Thus, he defends the fact that a poem is open to different interpretations which he considers as "all partial formulations of one thing."[3] He contends that "the ambiguities may be due to the fact that the poem means more, not less than ordinary speech can communicate" (*PP,* p. 23). Yet he maintains that "while poetry attempts to convey something beyond what can be conveyed in prose rhythms, it remains, all the same, one person talking to another; and this is just as true if you sing it, for singing is another way of talking" (*PP,* p. 23). These remarks of Eliot concerning the commonsense role of communication need to be kept in mind most particularly in evaluating his lyric poems. Of all forms the lyric has most to lose from the obscurity abounding in Eliot's early poetry.

The most cursory look at the Eliot corpus indicates that all of his poetry needs to be read with care; but the early poetry demands care of a different kind, or at least with a different emphasis, from that expended on the later works. From early to late Eliot's focus moves from the contemplation of ugliness toward transcending ugliness in the pursuit of beauty, and his style changes with the object of his contemplation. In *The Sacred Wood* (1920), written long before he started on the latter pursuit, Eliot commented on this natural process of changing emphasis: "The contemplation of the horrid or sordid or disgusting, by an artist, is the necessary and negative aspect of the impulse toward the pursuit of beauty. But not all succeed as did Dante in expressing the complete scale from negative to positive. The negative is the more importunate."[4] This importunate negative of Eliot's early poetry presents a problem which dogged his lyric verse of that period; namely, that of obscurity, which has annoyed some readers just as surely as it has charmed others. Whatever the individual reaction, no one denies the *fact* of Eliot's early obscurity, least of all Eliot himself.

In *The Use of Poetry,* written in the wake of his early poems, Eliot shows a tolerant attitude toward obscurity and unintelligible poetry. According to his analysis obscurity results from various causes, all of which apply to his early works. "First, there may be personal causes which make it impossible for a poet to express himself in any but an obscure way" (p. 143). Second, "The difficulty may be due just to novelty." Hostile critics found Wordsworth, Shelley, and Keats difficult but called them silly, thus making the new vulnerable to unwarranted ridicule. A third difficulty may be caused by a reader's expectation of obscurity. His guard against the difficult biases his receptivity and tends to obfuscate his sensitivity and openness to a new poem (p. 143).

With a kind of illogic that eludes explanation, certain readers of Eliot tend to cherish the early obscurity for its own sake, eschewing the later works, especially *Four Quartets,* precisely because they are too clear. The early obscurity seems to provide scope in this type of reader for what Eliot sees as "the desire to be clever and to look very hard for something, he doesn't know what–or else by the desire not to be taken in" (*UP,* p. 143). Eliot deserves a better audience. He is not guilty of what he calls, in "The Three Voices of Poetry," "the most bungling form of obscurity–that of the poet who has not been able to express himself to himself" (*PP,* p. 108). Nor does his poetry exhibit what he considers the "shoddiest form . . . when a poet is trying to persuade himself that he has something to say when he hasn't" (*PP,* p. 108).

It would be more just to give Eliot credit for trying "to put something into words which could not be said in any other way, and therefore in a language which may be worth the trouble of learning" (*PP,* p. 112). Cleanth Brooks refers to Eliot's stumbling block of obscurity as the problem of a "Discourse to the Gentiles,"[5] an attempt to get across a particular vision of reality to an audience which does not share with the poet a common repository of symbols which would constitute a kind of shorthand for that reality. No matter how necessary or justified obscurity is to Eliot's manner of writing, however, it nevertheless presents a formidable and particularly troublesome impediment to his lyric verse–a genre which demands an immediacy of perception, at least on one level of meaning. We see this drawback in some of the early lyrics, though it by no means destroys them as effective poems. On the other hand some of the clearest and most illuminating passages in the longer works, such as *The Waste Land* and "The Hollow Men," are in the short lyric intervals wherein one finds not only temporary respite from obscurity but also a positive illumination of some of the murky passages stretching before and after. An examination of the lyrical poems scattered through the *Collected Poems, 1909–1935* will give some idea of how far Eliot's lyric mastery was to develop.

In the subtitle for his Prufrock volume (1917), Eliot labels the whole collection as "observations," a word hardly associated at all with the lyric tradition and which consequently sets up no expectation for particularly lyrical poetry. Yet qualities endemic to the lyric tradition inform the entire volume in one way or another, sometimes holding a longer poem together, sometimes showing simply as a refrain in a generally prosaic poem.

"The Love Song of J. Alfred Prufrock" itself, in spite of its title, is a dramatic monologue rather than a song proper. Yet the title sets up no false expectation. While the monologue is certainly ironic, the touches of lyric grace throughout operate functionally to betray the romantic aspirations of the speaker and lend a whimsy and pathos to his abortive proposals. If J. Alfred Prufrock's aspirations are romantic, his view of himself as reflected from the world in which he moves is clinically hard, fixing him in a "formulated phrase." This contrast is the marrow of the poem, and the juxtaposition of lyricism with the tone of satire is the perfect vehicle for such tension. The musical features of "Prufrock" are obvious. The incantatory tone, the use of refrain and anaphora, are all evidence of an affinity with song indicated by the title. The title is not imposed as a joke. The music of the monologue bears it out, thus sustaining the irony while making it more subtle.

The outstanding feature of the music of "Prufrock" is the use of rime, profuse and haphazard, yet melodic. In no way, however, is it merely a decoration. Eliot's cadences are peppered with the ironic touch of rimed satire, especially notable in his coupling by rime words that, together, form a kind of absurdity. Thus the rime constitutes an implicit commentary on the ridiculous situation of the protagonist. Fittingly this satiric use of rime increases as the poem progresses and the speaker's view of his predicament becomes more clear. In the ninth verse paragraph satiric intent completely dominates the rime pattern. The stanza is punctuated by the middle and end rime "prayed-afraid." All the rest consist of such bits of levity as "ices-crisis," "platter-matter," "flicker-snicker," providing deflation by association, and thus showing Prufrock's pretensions in the merciless light of self-knowledge. Eliot's satiric use of rime does not have the uproarious bludgeon-blow effect of some of Dryden's rimes, nor the outlandish nonsensicalness of Byron's. J. Alfred Prufrock is too delicate a subject for the type of fun levelled at Richard Flecknoe or Donna Inez. But the kinship is obvious. The satiric use of rime in "Prufrock" is not divorced, however, from the more lyrical cadences dominating the poem. The difference is one of functional necessity, given the content and character of this particular monologue. Eliot uses his lyrical elements skillfully and with real decorum, lending a complicating dimension to a satiric portrait.

This is one use of lyricism in the early Eliot: to heighten the emotional tone of a nonlyric poem. It shows again in "Portrait of a Lady," not a lyric poem, yet enhanced by qualities belonging to a musical tradition. The use of rime and refrain, the progression of images through seasonal and diurnal change—all these features enhance the portrait, giving it emotional nuances not possible to attain without them. A line from the conclusion of the poem itself, though ironic, describes the melodic effect quite well: "This music is successful with a 'dying fall.' " The music preserves the tone of sophistication while carving out a delicacy of emotional detail needed to convey the uncertainty of feeling and thought in the protagonist. Eliot shows a particular predilection for this phrase "dying fall" which he has used for similar effect in "The Love Song of J. Alfred Prufrock": "I know the voices dying with a dying fall / Beneath the music from a farther room."

A somewhat different music starts to emerge in the "Preludes," composed of four separate pieces and terminated with a coda-like commentary tying all together. In these poems Eliot really attempts proper lyrics. This is noticeable especially in the first sketch and in the first half of the coda. The music in the other three is uneven and, fittingly, very much suppressed in the cynical commentary of the last three lines. For the first piece Eliot has devised a regular and carefully wrought system of metrics and rime. The four-stress lines are punctuated by two-stress ones after every pair, while the last four lines of the poem maintain the tetrameter uninterrupted. The rime scheme is in two parts, both matching in pattern, though the first is shorter than the last: *abcbdd efgfghh.* This first lyric is a sketch of the city at six o'clock in the evening with its familiar sights and smells. The picture is shabby but not sordid. The unevenness of the line span and the temporal irregularity of recurring rimes play down the careful structure Eliot has invented for the sketch. The rhythm thus fits a poem describing bits of newspaper and dead leaves blown about one's feet.

As the sketches succeed one another, the subject matter becomes progressively more sordid. As it does so, the music becomes less intricately structured. The consistent four-stress line and the haphazard use of rime are more prosaic vehicles, and convey the monotony and boredom of the unlovely lives depicted here. The first division of the coda is, once again, regular with its alternating 4-3, *ab* lines. It is in the first person, and the speaker expresses personal emotion provoked by his observations:

> I am moved by fancies that are curled
> Around these images, and cling:
> The notion of some infinitely gentle
> Infinitely suffering thing.

This is the only use of first person in the whole of the "Preludes," and the only indication of personal involvement by reaction to the scenes depicted.

Eliot uses a more musical regularity as a means of embodying the change of tone from detached observer to involved reactor. This emotional interrupter is immediately and finally eclipsed by the cynical conclusion:

> Wipe your hand across your mouth and laugh;
> The world revolves like ancient women
> Gathering fuel in vacant lots.

By contrast with the regularity of the first part of the coda, this conclusion is in a prosaic meter of unrimed verses. As he moves away from the speaker's personal expression into a cynical detachment, Eliot uses less musical regularity. Consciously or unconsciously he is in alignment with the lyric tradition in this.

To express the progressive revelation of futility in "Rhapsody on a Windy Night," Eliot applies a time sequence similar to the ones used in "Portrait of a Lady" and "Preludes." He employs systems of parallel imagery and, once more, a haphazard kind of rime which functions very well through the basically four-stress line pattern. In the last paragraph the metrics break up, moving from one-syllable to twelve-syllable lines and employing only one rime. The one-line coda, however, rimes with the last line of the closing paragraph: ". . . Put your shoes at the door, sleep, prepare for life / The last twist of the knife." The chiming of "knife" with "life" is ironic. The sequence of images sandwiched in by the sententious commands, "Mount" and "prepare for life," are pathetically commonplace and shabby, lending validity to and integrating the coda with the paragraph proper, and with all the preceding paragraphs depicting various scenes throughout the unlovely night. Eliot uses touches of rime and careful manipulation of metrics to convey varying tones and attitudes. Lyricism pervades these poems, emerging overtly when needed and receding when not. In Eliot the resurgence of lyricism in these symbolist pieces always indicates a heightening of emotion or the personal reaction of the protagonist to his observations. The observations take on a less objective tone by the poet's subtle manipulation of lyrical qualities.

After the imagistic detachment of the little sketch "Morning at the Window" with its suppressed music and tone of observation, the remainder of the first volume consists mainly of miniature character sketches. "The Boston Evening Transcript," "Aunt Helen," and "Cousin Nancy" are perhaps too ironic to be lyrical. "Mr. Apollinax," grinning like Beelzebub through the two-paragraph observation, is a puzzle. The grin inheres in the subject as well as the object. The speaker's irony is inimical to what we associate with lyric verse, and in this poem, as in the Boston portraits, the music is suppressed. In "Conversation Galante" Eliot plies a singsong regularity even more inimical to emotional seriousness than is a suppressed musical structure. The small talk and the sterility of the relationship depicted are mirrored deftly in the lightness and vacuity of the verse form.

"La Figlia che Piange" is another matter entirely. In the joining together of a subject and an attitude totally incongruous to each other, the speaker reveals his own character. One is reminded of Browning here. The subject is one of beauty and pain, a girl weeping as she is deserted by her lover. The speaker's attitude toward the scene is that of the clinical detachment of the aesthete. He thoroughly enjoys the attitude of the girl and mentally calls out stage directions:

> Stand on the highest pavement of the stair–
> Lean on a garden urn–
> Weave, weave the sunlight in your hair.

He relishes the "fugitive resentment" in her eyes and sunlight in her hair. The observation of passion as art has a tradition. Keats's "Ode on Melancholy" evidences a kind of heartless detachment in the lines:

> Or if thy mistress some rich anger shows
> Emprison her soft hand, and let her rave,
> And feed deep, deep upon her peerless eyes.[6]

The speaker's advice here is surely deficient as far as human relations go. It directs the lover to take pleasure in the girl's anger simply because it manifests a beauty not ordinarily experienced by him. There is no concern for the cause of the anger which might be painful to the subject.

Tennyson's sonnet "She took the dappled partridge flect with blood" is a more decadent manifestation of the same aesthetic urge. It takes deft artificiality for the speaker to make the best of an intrinsically ugly situation. He sees the girl as "a master-painting where she stood" with the bloody partridge dripping from her hands. He excuses her wanton act because it shows, to his perception at least, no aesthetic imperfection:

> Nor could I find an imperfection there,
> Nor blame the wanton act that showed so fair—
> To me whatever freak she plays is good.[7]

Because of this determination, the speaker salvages with his imagination the unlovely scene, and transforms it by a tour de force into aesthetic beauty. He observes the contrast of the bird's death and the girl's life, and claims that the latter

> Made quiet death so beautiful to see
> That Death lent grace to Life and Life to Death
> And in one image Life and Death repose.

Such a sense of beauty has to reside in the eye of the beholder, for it is most surely removed from the ordinary human response to the given situation.

Eliot's speaker in "La Figlia che Piange" shares the artistic detachment of Keats's and Tennyson's aesthetic lovers in the poems just cited. But his detachment goes much farther and is the more shocking. It provides by example a commentary on the aesthetic tradition of art for art's sake. The speaker's very sensitivity to beauty makes his attitude toward it seem all the more callous; and the fact that he is amazed and troubled by his own cogitations further emphasizes his degree of detachment as symptomatic. He does not wish the event to end happily: "I should have lost a gesture and a pose." He is able to abstract the gesture and pose from the emotion, and contemplate them as artifacts.

Eliot's craftsmanship in this poem is fine. He has produced a variation of dramatic monologue which is, for all its subtle complexity, truly a lyric —more so than the "Preludes" because it is more intensely emotional and more carefully rooted in musical regularity. The three stanzas are variations of a free use of alternating and coupling rime, with some of the rimes occurring after an interval of several lines. This suppression of rime lends a delicacy and subtlety suitable to the subject matter. In the first and last stanzas, which focus on the scene itself and the haunting memory of it, the musical base is more apparent. The second stanza, expressing the clinical objectivity of the speaker, is more prosaic in its rhythm, moving in lines from two to five feet in length with no pattern of change.

In this volume of "observations" Eliot employs qualities associated with the lyric tradition in a functional way as a form of shorthand to emphasize emotional elements, or as a means of revealing the inner nature of the speaker. He shows facility and a sense of fitness in all these practices. In a volume dominated by the dramatic monologue–a genre discussed in the preceding chapter as a special problem to lyric definition–Eliot shows a discriminating understanding of "the importance of *verse as speech* . . . and the importance of *verse as song.*"[8] In this quality, for which he praises Ezra Pound, Eliot himself exhibits real dexterity. He employs a "music of imagery and of sound,"[9] which resembles the rise, progress, and setting of imagery advocated by Keats as a lyric practitioner.

In both volumes, 1917 and 1920, one sees Eliot moving toward the long poem. Each volume is dominated by its respective "Prufrock" or "Gerontion." *Poems, 1920,* shows much less use for lyrical practice because it is less needed to fulfill the purposes of this volume. *Poems* consists of the long dramatic monologue "Gerontion"; six ironic pieces in tetrameter quatrains ("Burbank," "Sweeney Erect," "A Cooking Egg," "The Hippopotamus," "Whispers of Immortality," "Mr. Eliot's Sunday Morning Service"); four French poems; and "Sweeney among the Nightingales." The poems are scoffing and more humorous than those of the 1917 volume. The quatrain dominates with its singsong iambic tetrameter and alternating rime–a form Eliot abandoned after this volume. A particularly unlyrical verse form in Eliot's hands, it is well suited for the tone of the 1920 collection, so different from the rest of his work.

The *Ariel Poems,* which follow upon the three longer works, *The Waste Land* (1922), "The Hollow Men" (1925), and "Ash Wednesday" (1930), are much more indicative of the line of development Eliot was to take. Of the *Ariel Poems* three are dramatic monologues of high lyric intensity. "Animula" is too generalized and ruminatory to be considered as lyric verse; "The Cultivation of Christmas Trees" is too deliberately prosaic in tone. The three more lyrical monologues vary considerably in their musical structures. The first two are based on biblical accounts, but "Journey of the Magi" relies on the prose rhythms of Lancelot Andrewes to set the tone, while "A Song for Simeon" follows the rhythms of the *nunc dimittis* in its dignified serenity. For "Marina" Eliot uses the dream-vision lyricism employed a few months earlier in "Ash Wednesday," from which the monologue derives in subject and tone.

While "Journey of the Magi" gets under way with the taut prose of Lancelot Andrewes, the lines become more relaxed and the images more symbolic as the poem progresses. In the last verse paragraph the speaker is once more in the present time, and there is an immediacy to his diction which does not belong to the two preceding sections that recount the past. Eliot, by quoting Andrewes, starts the poem with verse as speech and never really moves into verse as song. But there is no speech exactly like this of the old Magus. His speech admirably mirrors in its rhythm and images the emotional impact of the past experience and its subsequent transformation of the present. Eliot uses no rime, but falling line cadence is discernible, especially in the first two verse paragraphs recounting the time relived in memory, time eternally transformed by the encounter there recorded. The present time, made hard by contrast, is less musical in its line cadence. The falling rhythm is in good part replaced by insistent monosyllabic line endings, in which the word "death" predominates.

It is a music invented for the purpose of this monologue, and admirably represents the spoken word. It is lyrical, to be sure, but its lyricism is certainly not that of the sung lyric. For "A Song for Simeon" Eliot employs an altogether different music. Structurally the poem is divided into four shorter verse paragraphs of greater regularity. Eliot employs rime in loose pattern and a basically masculine line ending through the first two paragraphs. The lines have an unmistakably biblical cadence and tone, infusing the monologue with the dignity of its source. Once again the last paragraph, like its parallel in "Journey of the Magi," makes a notable shift in sound structure. The second half of the poem relies on increasing use of falling rhythm at line ends, coinciding with the vision of suffering therein expressed. In addition to this separation of rhythmic quality between the first and the last halves of the poem, there is also a marked breakdown of line regularity between the last two paragraphs. The penultimate paragraph is sonorous and serene, giving grandeur to the vision of ultimate Crucifixion. When Simeon dissociates himself from the vocation implied in the Crucifixion of the Word of God, he uses intonation that separates the music of dismissal from that of participation. The last paragraph maintains the dignity while reinforcing the weariness of the old prophet and his longing for honorable dismissal from his watch. Like Moses on Mount Nebo he fulfills his vocation in living to *see* the ultimate vision, not to partake of it. Yet Simeon's role is not without vicarious participation: "I am tired with my own life and the lives of those after me, / I am dying in my own death and the deaths of those after me." His final departure is not the bowing out of one who has made the ultimate refusal, but of one who has fulfilled his role as seer: "Let thy servant depart / Having seen thy salvation." The prophet, as seer, has his vision, a vision that has caused him pain by the knowledge it has imparted, though it is not experiential knowledge in the sense of the Magi's. The vision of Simeon overlaps that of the Magus. He refers to "this birth season of decease," just as the Magus reflects that "this Birth was / Hard and bitter agony for us, like Death, our death." The difference is one of direct experience as opposed to indirect. Both experiences have imparted a rare kind of after-vision.

This idea of knowledge leading to death and ultimate resurrection is central to Eliot. It appears earlier in *The Waste Land* and "Gerontion" and runs through his works into "Ash Wednesday" and *Four Quartets.* An extraordinarily beautiful variation of the theme is found in "Marina," the last of the original *Ariel Poems.* "Marina," of all the *Ariel Poems,* most resembles "Ash Wednesday" in mood and music. It was written after the longer poem, and the influence is seen most strikingly in the intercessory figure. Pericles is restored through Marina, as Dante is through Beatrice, humankind through thc Virgin Mary. What the hyacinth girl could not do in *The Waste Land* is effected here through the presence of the lost daughter. This mysterious importance of place and the need of human encounter for the dispensing of grace are at the heart of Eliot's thematic development. In "Ash Wednesday" and "Marina" the theme is given intense lyric expression. Because this theme is integral in Eliot's development as a lyric poet, "Marina" is given extensive treatment here.

F. O. Matthiessen, echoing something Eliot has said about Dante (*SE,* p. 237), observes of "Ash Wednesday": "Of all Eliot's poems 'Ash Wednesday' would have the best chance of appealing to an audience that could neither read nor write."[10] This could be applied as well to "Marina." To quote Matthiessen further: "Even though the feelings which he is expressing are extremely complex, and the sequence of his thought by no means easy to follow, it nevertheless remains true that on its first hearing the poem is capable of making an instantaneous impression through the beauty of its sound" (p. 114). What constitutes the beauty of the sound in "Marina" is not easy to pin down. Like the meaning, it is not immediately apprehensible. It is, nonetheless, a bewitching kind of music that leads unmistakably to the gradual comprehension of the meaning. There is no trick involved. Eliot has always been an affirmed advocate of Pope's principle: "The Sound should seem an echo to the Sense." Nor is he haphazard about its application. He observes that "the music of poetry is not something which exists apart from the meaning" (*PP,* p. 21). In reversing an earlier evaluation of Milton, Eliot notes that "the music of verse is strongest in poetry which has a definite meaning expressed in the properest words."[11] When the "definite meaning" happens to involve the mystery of grace and presence, it is difficult to find the "properest words" without risking some elusiveness. This is the problem Eliot has to cope with in "Marina."

In "The Music of Poetry" (1942) Eliot notes that "there are poems in which we are moved by the music and take the sense for granted, just as there are poems in which we attend to the sense and are moved by the music without noticing it" (*PP,* p. 21). Neither is quite the case with "Marina." The music and sense are interdependent, and one cannot speak of either one in isolation from the other. In noting two extremes within the range of poetry—poems which direct the reader's attention to either sound or sense in separation—Eliot remarks: ". . . with either type, sound and sense must cooperate; in even the most purely incantatory poems, the dictionary meanings of words cannot be disregarded with impunity."[12] Eliot is consistent in this principle of the inseparability of sound and sense—a principle inherent in the lyric tradition.

Perhaps his clearest statement on this is in "The Music of Poetry" where he insists

> that a "musical poem" is a poem that has a musical pattern of sound and a musical pattern of secondary meanings of words which compose it, and that these two patterns are indissoluble and one. And if you object that it is only the pure sound, apart from the sense, to which the adjective "musical" can be rightly applied, I can only reaffirm my previous assertion that the sound of a poem is as much an abstraction from the poem as is the sense. (*PP*, p. 26)

In writing about Rilke in 1955 Eliot admits a temptation to enjoy the verbal beauty of the *Duinese Elegies,* to be moved by the music in abstraction and not enter the thought which he finds uncongenial and difficult.[13] But he considers this a flaw in his own reading inclination, and not the proper way to approach Rilke.

For purposes of analysis, of course, a critic must deal with sound and sense in abstraction, but this is only a process leading to a final synthesis for further appreciation or understanding. Herein lies an occupational hazard for the close reader. His analysis can destroy the enjoyment of a poem by selective perception. Eliot calls it a problem of the ear:

> . . . and by "ear" for poetry I mean an immediate apprehension of two things which can be considered in abstraction from each other, but which produce their effect in unity: rhythm and diction. They imply each other: for the diction—the vocabulary and construction—will determine the rhythm, and the rhythms which a poet finds congenial will determine his diction.[14]

"Marina" exemplifies this principle in its particular way of achieving verbal beauty through integration of rhythm and diction. One is struck by the softness of the vowel and consonant sounds, the frequent use of falling cadence, the continual recurrence of anaphora and epiphora in phrase and line structures. The tone quality of the poem is consistent in all but the second paragraph on the seven deadly sins, a passage which needs for contrast a hard regularity and solidity of construction. The extreme simplicity of the diction is impressive, for that diction embodies images of power and great beauty. These images, moreover, are "plotted" in a Keatsian sense, producing what Eliot called "a musical pattern of emotional overtones."[15]

The images move through a temporal sequence from present to past, then to a new present in which the past is restored and the future is held implicitly. Time is transcended by the infiltration of grace through the restoration of the daughter lost at sea.

The poem, in seven irregular paragraphs, opens with the awakening of the protagonist to the "higher dream" of "Ash Wednesday." By the intercessory figure—here the daughter—the old man's senses and spirit are inundated with new life through a transforming understanding of reality. The nature of the perception is that of experiential knowledge channelled through the physical place. Eliot has made the terms of the vision concrete in the materialistic tradition of orthodox Christian theology on the Resurrection. But Eliot wraps his theology in a fresh particularity and the poignancy of lyric expression. In so doing he gives to the visionary experience described a solid dimension and authenticity.

The intercessory figure, moreover, is not some nebulous unreality. If the daughter is strange in restoration, she is nevertheless real and particular. If recognition is gradual, it is sure:

> What is this face, less clear and clearer
> The pulse in the arm, less strong and stronger—
> Given or lent? more distant than stars and
> nearer than the eye.

She restores to her father the past filled with "Whispers and small laughter between leaves and hurrying feet." She imparts a true vision of the present and the material of his life with its "Bowsprit cracked with ice and paint cracked with heat." Her presence brings the grace that impregnates past and present with a new life to which the old man resigns himself:

> let me
> Resign my life for this life, my speech for that unspoken,
> The awakened, lips parted, the hope, the new ships.

The renewal of life in the father through the daughter, lost at sea and restored by the sea, is a spiritual one, enveloping the material and transforming it. Thus it is an incremental restoration, multilevelled and intense. This is not an easy subject. To convey a sense of such experience is a difficult task, and Eliot uses language with discretion and fine craftsmanship. In an essay on "Swinburne as Poet" (1920), Eliot made some careful discriminations among values in language, coming to the conclusion that "the language which is more important to us is that which is struggling to digest and express new objects, . . . new feelings, new aspects. . . ." (*SE,* p. 285).

This is precisely the problem of communication Eliot is faced with in a poem concerning beatitude. Pericles' confrontation with reality is more mysterious than Simeon's situation and attitude, yet Eliot does manage to commit to language a powerful sense of the mystery.

Eliot effects this by small, sure strokes of sound control and precise, unpretentious diction. He has in "Marina" an absolute control of his auditory imagination, making the reader experience the power of the poem before the full meaning becomes clear. Nowhere so far in his shorter poems does Eliot depend so strongly on his use of sound for conveyance of meaning. In the *Use of Poetry* he defines the auditory imagination as

> the feeling for syllable and rhythm, penetrating far below the conscious levels of thought and feeling, invigorating every word; sinking to the most primitive and forgotten, returning to the origin and bringing something back, seeking the beginning and the end. It works through meaning, certainly, or not without meanings in the ordinary sense, and fuses the old and obliterated and the trite, the current, and the new and surprising, the most ancient and the most civilized mentality." (P. 111)

It seems that through his auditory imagination Eliot manifests something of the quality he praises in Dante: the ability to make us apprehend sensuously at least one aspect or stage of blessedness—the initial acceptance of its penetration. He praises Dante for his power of making us realize at every moment "the inapprehensible in visual images."[16]

His task in "Marina" is of smaller scale but analogous. For Eliot the task is particularly difficult because the material is not sympathetic to his contemporaries: "We have (whether we know it or not) a prejudice against beatitude as material for poetry" (*SE*, p. 225). Yet it is in handling this difficult material or its prerequisite of purgation that Eliot is most lyrical. It is as if he needs to rely heavily on the music for intensity. Eliot is aware of the power inherent in lyrical verse. Praising Valéry for his emphasis on structure, he notes that the French poet "always maintained that assimilation of Poetry to Music which was a Symbolist tenet."[17] For Eliot music had a special value among the arts: "Music itself may be conceived as striving towards an unattainable timelessness; as if the other arts may be thought of as yearning for duration, so music may be thought of as yearning for the stillness of painting or sculpture" (p. xiv).

It is to capture the stillness of beatitude breaking into time that Eliot frequently employs lyric poetry. "Ash Wednesday" is a notable example among the longer poems. Helen Gardner notes that the style of "Ash Wednesday" is "exactly opposite of a rhetorical style. . . . It is a lyrical style, and in 'Ash Wednesday' Mr. Eliot reaches what he rarely attained before, the peculiar poignancy of lyric utterance."[18] The peculiar poignancy running through "Ash Wednesday" spills over in a marked way into "Marina," the only one of the original *Ariel Poems* to be written after it.

The handful of lyrics that comprise *Minor Poems* contains some fine examples of Eliot's work in the genre. "Five-Finger Exercises" move from the delicate whimsy of a child's world and the language of nursery rimes to the irreverent jingles on Ralph Hodgson and the clerically trim Mr. Eliot himself. As one would expect, the more satiric pieces are less lyrical, and the shift in mood is happily signalled by Eliot's swipe at Tennyson in "Lines to a Duck in the Park." These are delightful poems exemplifying something Eliot noted about Edward Lear's verse: "We enjoy the music, which is of a high order, and we enjoy the feeling of irresponsibility towards the sense" (*PP,* p. 21). It is a poetry of relaxation, and the music brings about such an effect. Of course, *Old Possum's Book of Practical Cats* is the supreme example of Eliot's gift with nonsense verse.

The five "Landscapes" are very effective lyrics, showing artistic control in the correspondence of sound to sense, and one guesses that these poems gave the author a good bit of delight in the making. More important, however, is the light they can give on Eliot's development toward *Four Quartets* in the use of place for lyric subject matter. In each scene of "Landscapes" neither the speaker nor the chosen hearer is very clearly particularized. What comes across is the speaker's meditation on the place observed; his message is an outcome of this meditation. "New Hampshire," a reflection on the human age that comes "Between the blossom- and the fruit-time," is loaded with Edenic symbols of weighty significance. Yet the poem preserves the simple, primitive attitude of children at their outdoor games. Eliot's easy use of synecdoche and onomatopoeic imagery carries the poem, whose music contrasts sharply with the impeded flow of the red river in "Virginia."

In the latter poem heat, motionless and oppressive, is concretized in the silent landscape and the river sluggish with its load of ore. In addressing the river the speaker comments with a fascinating image: "Slow flow heat is silence." The perception of heat is further intensified by the question:

> Will heat move
> Only through the mocking bird
> Heard once?

Eliot's selection of detail here is astute. The only sign of life is the bird's call, and the bird has not enough energy to put forth its voice more than once. The play on the word "will" at the beginning and the reference to "Iron thoughts" at the end give to the sketch a human significance raising it above a mere landscape. But the landscape itself is powerful. The impeded motion of the river is exemplified in the images and reinforced by a sound-structure marked with monosyllables, two-word sentences, and repetition of words reinforced by internal chiming. In a sense it is a companion to the free swinging action of the children in the appletree who inhabited the preceding landscape.

"Usk" is a more quiet poem than either. The voice becomes the Tiresian prophet-like voice in *The Waste Land.* Its admonition is a familiar one for the Eliot reader. Old enchantments are to be put away with the rimes of nursery games. The way to be sought is that of "The hermit's chapel, the pilgrim's prayer"—the Chapel Perilous of *The Waste Land,* the saint's stair of "Ash Wednesday." Again the sound is admirably suited to the sense. Eliot here uses couplet rimes which triple on the last three verses. The rime adds a certain sententiousness, yet it does not become overbearing because of the varying line lengths in which the rime sequences occur.

"Rannoch, by Glencoe" forms a powerful commentary on defeat and blood lust. It is a kind of disgrace dissolved in place, for it is in the details selected from the scene that the speaker gets across his perception of futility, and the irony of the long-lived endurance of memory to preserve spiritual pain beyond the grave. All the features of the landscape embody the futility of human pride defeated: the starving crow, the patient stag awaiting the rifle. Again Eliot evidences extraordinary ability to concretize a spiritual state in landscape images:

Between the soft moor
And the soft sky, scarcely room
To leap or soar.

The word "soft" reinforces the onomatopoeic structure, surely; but more important, it gives a kinetic conception of the confinement of the spirit in a miasmic milieu where nothing can support the aspirations of man. The poem is pervaded with the "listlessness" and "languor" of inglorious defeat and ignoble victory in the "Clamour of confused wrong." The art of selection and condensation carries the emotion of the commentary, and this is reinforced by skillful use of onomatopoeia, soft consonant sounds, sibilants, and liquids. Only in the last four lines, where the speaker is commenting on the power of memory, does he employ harder sounds: "Beyond the bone. Pride snapped . . . / No concurrence of bone." Sound-structure changes in order to correspond to the nuance in meaning. Neither Campbell nor MacDonald can rest in the outcome.

The last of the landscapes, "Cape Ann," is a sheer delight of tonal dexterity. Eliot makes marvellous use of the names of birds and their actions as the base of his music. Note the speed with which the reader's attention flits from one bird flight to the next, corresponding to the speed of each bird's coming on and off the observer's span of vision. The reader's perception is controlled by the speaker's. The grammar of the poem reinforces this with its many imperatives. The dominant command is "Follow," and this is exactly what the reader is impelled to do. One gets the sense of great agility on Eliot's part and great ease and mastery in the manipulation of sound. These landscapes would exemplify Eliot's caution concerning sound as imitation of instrumental music,[19] did not the sound-structures make so much sense. The music of these short pieces does for "Landscapes" what the melody does for a sung lyric. It is indispensable if the full meaning is to be grasped.

Just as "The Love Song of J. Alfred Prufrock" dominates the 1917 volume, and "Gerontion" the 1920 collection, the dream lyric "Eyes that last I saw in tears" leads the *Minor Poems* with a rare and penetrating use of lyricism. Though a minor poem, it will be given extensive treatment here for two reasons. In technique the poem illustrates an accomplished rendering of the best principles of lyric verse. Even more important is the fact that the poem has never been fully explicated, and the subject matter is crucial in tracing the direction Eliot was to take in his selection of material for his lyric poetry. He moves more and more into a preoccupation with human response as the basis of human beatitude. "Eyes that last I saw in tears" deals with this material powerfully and provocatively with intense lyric grace.

This poem and the one following it, "The wind sprang up at four o'clock," were both rejects from "The Hollow Men," and indeed would have changed the complexion of that poem had they been left in their respective places in parts 2 and 4. It is fortunate, however, that Eliot chose to preserve them elsewhere. Both lyrics deal with that Virgilian twilight zone between spiritual death ("death's dream kingdom") and death proper ("death's other Kingdom"). Both involve a transformed vision of the reality that has made up one's life—transformed by the kind of self-knowledge that comes in an after-life evaluation. The concept of reevaluation of one's past action is especially poignant in "Eyes that last I saw in tears," which has its roots in the sixth book of the *Aeneid.*

The pious Aeneas, so sure in the conscious direction of his gods when he sailed from Carthage, and enabled by that sureness to numb his consciousness to the light from the funeral pyre receding behind him, is much less secure when he encounters Dido in the Underworld. His "Sed me iussa deum" is lame and seems not to hold much conviction under the scrutiny of Dido's disregarding presence. The incident is archetypal and can be universalized into a symbol of culpable failure in human relations, so often attributed to circumstances or "powers beyond one's control." For Aeneas it is obedience to the gods who have destined him for Rome and Lavinia, a native wife; for the man in the hyacinth garden it is the paralysis that comes from looking into the heart of light.

Eliot is fascinated by the significance of the scene in book 6 and ponders its layered meanings in both his essays on Virgil (1944 and 1951).[20] It is worth quoting Eliot at length on this Virgilian material because of the importance his reflections have to his practice of the lyric. In the first he writes:

> . . . I have always thought the meeting of Aeneas with the shade of Dido, in Book VI, not only one of the most poignant, but one of the most civilized passages in poetry. It is complex in meaning and economical in expression, for it not only tells us about the attitude of Aeneas. Dido's behaviour appears almost as a projection of Aeneas' own conscience: this, we feel, is the way in which Aeneas' conscience would *expect* Dido to behave to him. The point, it seems to me, is not that Dido is unforgiving—though it is important that, instead of railing at him, she merely snubs him—perhaps the most telling snub in all poetry: what matters most is, that Aeneas does not forgive himself—and this, significantly, in spite of the fact of which he is well aware, that all he has done has been in compliance with destiny, or in consequence of the machinations of the gods who are in themselves, we feel, only instruments of a greater inscrutable power. (*PP*, pp. 63–64)

Eliot considered the Virgilian passage a sophisticated testimonial to "civilized consciousness and conscience." All his own serious poetry is a probing of this conscience, and all his markedly lyric verse is a contemplation of some kind of moment of encounter with reality as a moment of grace. As the individual responds to this grace, he is either fixed in an attitude of refusal or transformed by the motion of acceptance. Eliot is haunted by the spiritual death of those who have made "the great refusal," and the intensified life of those who have accepted the creative diminishment of total response to others.

In his second essay on Virgil, Eliot notes a curious lack in the Roman poet. Eliot's observation points up his own ideas concerning the value of love as "the cause and end of movement" ("Burnt Norton" 5) in human life and destiny:

> The term which one can justifiably regret the lack of in Virgil is *amor.* It is, above all others, the key word for Dante. I do not mean that Virgil never uses it. . . . Certainly, the love of Aeneas and Dido has great tragic force. There is tenderness and pathos enough in the *Aeneid.* But Love is never given, to my mind, the same significance as a principle of order in the human soul, in society and in the universe that *pietas* is given; and it is not Love that causes *fatum* or moves the sun and the stars. (*PP*, pp. 147–48)

For Eliot, of course, destiny *is* caused by love or its denial. His reflections on the lack of the quality in Aeneas are not limited to the great refusal depicted in *Aeneid* 4 and punished by conscience concretized in Dido's snub of book 6. The theme is everywhere in Eliot.

Eliot's minor lyric "Eyes that last I saw in tears" is a poignant variation on the Dido-Aeneas theme. The speaker inhabits "death's dream kingdom" and is haunted by the very memory of the division enacted in the past. The tears rendered at that time are now gone, and he must face the "Eyes of decision" which no longer weep over wrong done, but inflict their own form of pain in retribution. They are eyes of judgment which mercilessly reflect the speaker's judgment of self. He undergoes "the rending pain of re-enactment" mentioned in "Little Gidding." The derision in which the eyes hold him reflects the speaker's own futile self-knowledge acquired too late and to no purpose, for it effects no change. It is an adumbration of the kind of deprivation he will suffer in "death's other Kingdom." His will is already fixed, and the outcome is an extension of the moment of refusal indicating a habit of refusal which will issue in an eternity of isolation. His present knowledge does not transform the past as in "Marina" or as hinted in "Gerontion" and *The Waste Land.* Gerontion can say with well-founded remorse: "I that was near your heart was removed therefrom / To lose beauty in terror, terror in inquisition." He is an old man waiting for rain, nonetheless; and he is directly addressing Christ as other. With Pericles it is a more definitely salvific orientation: ". . . let me / Resign my life for this life . . . the hope, the new ships."

The speaker in "Eyes that last I saw in tears" uses first person throughout but it is not a private situation. Like Gerontion, the speaker can be each of us. The subtle use of allusion to *Aeneid* 6 enriches the poem and gives it dimension only because it is already a universal situation. The allusion, if recognized, gives the poem a specificity, but a specificity that transcends the particular incident it recalls. Thus the sudden shift to first person plural in the last line of Eliot's lyric seems a perfectly natural outcome of the vision imparted. Given a bit more depth and sensitivity, the young man in "Portrait of a Lady" or the observer in "La Figlia che Piange" could come to such a vision.

It is a situation par excellence for the lyric, and Eliot uses it repeatedly. The lines from "The Hollow Men" summarize the situation quite well:

> Between the emotion
> And the response
> Falls the Shadow.

In "Eyes that last I saw in tears" the diction is simple, the emotion intense, the rhythm delicate, the rime discreet, the images general. Eliot handles the unpretentious ingredients with maximum skill to produce an excellent music. Note, for example, the two leading words "eyes" and "tears" in the dominant positions at beginnings and ends of lines. He uses them with emotional force and vigor without becoming maudlin. No adjective is needed as a crutch. The eyes are described by their power to move the speaker.

The two stanzas comprising the poem are linked structurally by the repetition of "This is my affliction." The first stanza focuses on the present, "death's dream kingdom"; the second on the extension of consciousness into "death's other Kingdom" where the vision of self, as reflected in the eyes of another, is fixed forever. The movement is carefully signalled in the progression of another prominent word pattern in the feminine rimes: "division," "affliction," "decision," "derision." The progression from "division" to "derision" is devastating, yet executed with a verbal economy that underpins its strength.

One sees in Eliot's work a continual flow of lyric verse broken only in the 1920 collection of witty satiric verse, a volume that seems an aberration from his natural base in serious emotional content. The highlights are scattered throughout the period stretching from 1911 to 1935 and are impressive. The more successful the lyric, the greater its clarity. None of his poems is easy, and each poses special problems within lyric categorization. The "Preludes" are too objective; "La Figlia che Piange" is distanced from its emotional subject by the rhetorical structure. While the *Ariel Poems* are dramatic monologues of a high order, and "Marina" in particular is intense in emotion and powerful in melody, yet the form itself poses a problem. The "Landscapes" of the mid-thirties are noticeably different from the "Preludes" written in 1915 as far as lyric method is concerned. The speaker is much more moved by the scene, and communicates the emotional effect of the landscapes by a perfect command of music.

It seems that, as Eliot grew in maturity as a poetic practitioner, he allowed more emotional expression and found the right, the precise way to commit that expression to words. Surely the intensity and control are splendid in "Eyes that last I saw in tears," written in 1924. Eliot's astute use of allusion is a marvel of economy in the conveyance of direct emotion and the wider human significance of the incident portrayed. At this period Eliot relies on a Virgilian twilight atmosphere for good reason. What he deals with is the mystery of encounter, the mystery of the transforming impact of other on the self. "Ash Wednesday" and "Marina" treat of the encounter accepted and responded to; "Eyes that last I saw in tears" records the attitude of one who had made the great refusal, and knows what has been and what is to follow from that action. Such things are mysteries and cannot be formulated with ease. One must grope for the proper expression, and Eliot is confronted with a Protean wrestle with words in trying to convey what he perceives in those mysteries. The effect is at once powerful and nebulous. One is affected by the music before he totally perceives the meaning. The meaning dawns gradually and never in isolation from the music. One perceives how the sound embodies the sense; it is the flesh and bones of the meaning structure. The method weaves an unmistakable aura of mystery which, in these poems, is very much to the purpose.

Later Eliot alters his style, though the subject matter continues more and more to deal with the sacramental nature of encounter and commitment "to another, or to others, or to God." The sacredness of place as a channel for encounter is another idea that continues to take shape in Eliot. Pericles experiences his daughter through a "grace dissolved in place"; the protagonist of "Burnt Norton" recounts his experience of reality by indicating the place where the experience was granted: "I can only say, *there* we have been: but I cannot say where / And I cannot say, how long, for that is to place it in time."

The *Four Quartets,* all named after definite places, are not confined to the physical limitations of those places. When one is at Burnt Norton or Little Gidding, one cannot say *where* he has been. The place partakes of the experience, and that experience transcends both place and time: "Here, the intersection of the timeless moment / Is England and nowhere. Never and always." This, to be sure, is difficult subject matter, no less than was the early material for his lyric poems. But the *Four Quartets* are easier to read. They are clear in a way the earlier poems could not afford to be without losing the mystery essential to their meaning. The quartets in no way slight the element of mystery, but somehow manage to cope with expressing mystery in a language of lucid simplicity and lyric competence which surpasses his earlier works. The poems are dense but not obscure.

CHAPTER THREE

LYRICISM IN THE LONGER POEMS: *THE WASTE LAND,* "THE HOLLOW MEN," "ASH WEDNESDAY"

It would be useful to examine Eliot's functional development of lyricism through the longer, separately published poems (*The Waste Land,* 1922; "The Hollow Men," 1925; and "Ash Wednesday," 1930), before developing this point as it is exemplified with great lyric clarity in *Four Quartets* proper.

Though the shorter poem is more amenable to the demands of the lyric tradition, we see lyric qualities operating in the longer works. The muted music of "The Hollow Men" marks the poem with unmistakable lyricism. *The Waste Land* depends on lyrical qualities to give full impact to such scenes as the hyacinth garden, Elizabeth and Leicester in the barge, the Thames-daughters, "Death by Water," Gethsemane and Calvary at the opening of the last section. The all-pervading lyricism of "Ash Wednesday" was referred to briefly in the treatment of "Marina" in the preceding chapter (cf. pp. 20–24) and will be pointed out in more detail here. The point is that in all these cases a definite correspondence exists between Eliot's desire to convey intense emotional experience and his use of lyricism in the poems. But his employment of the techniques of lyricism here is markedly different from that in *Four Quartets.* In his earlier long poems Eliot employs lyric material as interludes and intensifiers of the various ideas under consideration. In "Ash Wednesday" the entire idea eludes rational expression, and the whole fabric of the poem is lyrical. Thus, as Eliot progresses from *The Waste Land* to "Ash Wednesday," his lyricism becomes more pervasive and more varied in function from poem to poem. In all three cases, moreover, it differs from the lyricism that will emerge in *Four Quartets.*

THE WASTE LAND

From the lyrical opening of *The Waste Land* to the closing refrain, Eliot uses structural and verbal music to heighten a sense of emotional awareness. From time to time memory and desire encroach upon a world peopled by the spiritually dead. These intrusions are always lyrical in tone, but are not distillations of the scenes or passages at hand. Rather they are in opposition and stand out from the context, thus forming a tension between real life and the kind of nonlife which Eliot scrutinizes.

The opening seven lines of "The Burial of the Dead" are a powerful exposition of the state of spiritual death: the speaker wishes to be left alone, not wanting the intrusion of life in any form. One is struck immediately by the heavy, falling cadence, intensified by the irony of the diction. That unwanted, unsolicited, disruptive intrusion of life is met with nonresponse by the comfortable dead. Eliot achieves a sense of irony in the tensions between life and death. The protagonist perceives life as undesirable; the reader, through the self-revelation of the protagonist, perceives his state of spiritual death as undesirable. The diction, heavily weighted with images of life, mirrors the protagonist's feeling of burdensomeness at this intrusion. The heavily falling rhythm intensifies this sense of active pressure met with passive resistance. Eliot's placement of caesuras before the end participles gives emphasis to these very active words: "breeding," "mixing," "stirring," "covering," "feeding." The words are further strengthened by being in an enjambed position. The state of spiritual stagnation that leavens the poem is confronted by moments of vision when life is present as a costly and mysterious alternative. The opening lines create that tension which will from time to time disturb the inhabitants of the wasteland throughout the entire poem.

The first such intrusion comes after the biblical voice invites us to "Come in under the shadow of this red rock" in order to experience "fear in a handful of dust." Abruptly the focus shifts to the hyacinth garden, the scene of a failure of love. The passage is in the form of a lyrical dialogue wherein the participants, ironically, do not communicate. The hyacinth girl is described in terms of fertility symbols: arms full of flowers, hair wet from the garden. She is all life. In spite of his perception of life in the girl confronting him, the respondent can speak only to himself. His speech mirrors his emotional incapacity. "Looking into the heart of light, the silence" has taken away his powers of speech and sight, of mind and soul. In contrast to the hyacinth girl, he is "neither / Living nor dead" and knows nothing. His state vibrates with that of Gerontion:

I that was near your heart was removed therefrom
To lose beauty in terror, terror in inquisition.
I have lost my passion . . .
I have lost my sight, smell, hearing, taste and touch:
How should I use them for your closer contact?

This mysterious failure to love places the speaker in the hyacinth garden in a spiritual wasteland with all the others who need burial or death by water. The passage is given considerable richness by its careful placement between the two Wagnerian fragments.

Wagner's *Tristan und Isolde* opens, after the prelude, with the young sailor's lyric from which Eliot lifts the middle lines:

Frisch weht der Wind
Der Heimat zu
Mein Irisch Kind,
Wo weilest du?

Wagner's sailor is tuneful in a musical milieu of gorgeous dissonance, simple in a love-maze of labyrinthine perplexity. His lines are a fitting introduction to the words of the hyacinth girl. They show a fresh and uncomplicated love, simple and innocent. But in both settings the lines are ironic. The words of the sailor, singing to his Irish sweetheart, awaken the ill-fated Isolde, who thinks she is being mocked. She then unfolds her stormy tale of what she believes to be her betrayal by Tristan into a one-sided love. Isolde's tumultuous outburst displays a landscape of the distraught mind where all is out of joint because of unreciprocal love. Her tale is framed by the song of the sailor, who breaks in once again, innocently from his perch on the high mast, when Isolde finishes. Eliot's hyacinth garden episode is framed on one side by this happy song and on the other by the desolate lines from act 3 when Tristan, dying from his wounds and waiting for Isolde to come and heal him, is told that no ship is in sight: "Oed' und leer das Meer" (Desolate and void the sea).

This is a fine example of Eliot's manipulation of sources for his particular ends. By selecting lyrical fragments from acts 1 and 3 of *Tristan und Isolde*, he not only heightens the intensity of the emotions which he so sparsely portrays, but also telescopes, by association, a desolate ending for his hyacinth scene. Thus Eliot condenses by his allusion the entire tragic course of the opera, but without its tragic grandeur and the eternal fidelity of the lovers beyond the bounds of death. His selectivity forces on the reader's perception a comparison of his lovers with those of the myth. The man in the hyacinth garden is damned by this comparison. Eliot's use of Wagner's "Oed' und leer das Meer" is a fitting close to a passage that depicts emotional paralysis in the face of emotional promise:

> I could not
> Speak, and my eyes failed, I was neither
> Living nor dead, and I knew nothing,
> Looking into the heart of light, the silence.

The hyacinth incident is a breath of the promise of what might be in a world oppressed by acedia. The inhabitants are like those outside Dante's first circle of Hell who never were alive: "che mai non fur vivi" (*Inferno* 3.61). The incident of promise and refusal intrudes between the "stony rubbish" of the desert scene preceding it and the sterile wasteland of Madame Sosostris and her circle of clients. The passage is set off by its lyrical tone from the dry passages before and after. It serves as a measure for the emotional sterility of the whole section in which it occurs.

"A Game of Chess" has no lyrical passages per se, but there is exquisite music in the Keatsian description of opulence at the opening of the first scene. The richness of the material setting only serves to elucidate the spiritual poverty of the wealthy couple who speak at each other without communicating.

In the dialogue which follows the opening description, Eliot uses two lyric touches to emphasize the distance between the two speakers. The "Shakespeherian Rag" serves the purpose of ironic flippancy which discloses a frustration in the man who, in this vapid situation, can still remember "Those are pearls that were his eyes." The line from "Full fathom five . . ." brings with it by association the whole of Ariel's lyric and the whole meaning of *The Tempest* which this lyric epitomizes. It is a brief and powerful rapier thrust of memory, but it has no strength to stir. Its intensity is heightened by the ironic flippancy of the "Shakespeherian Rag" that dismisses the brief insight from present consciousness. Just as the Dantesque language and the Wagnerian fragments underscore the sense of what is lost in the hyacinth garden, so here the Shakespearean allusion intensifies by contrast the hollowness of the speakers. Their inner landscape is indeed a desert of "empty cisterns and exhausted wells."

The marital situation in the second scene is no better. For the tawdry narration about Lil and Albert by their friend in the public house, Eliot uses no lyric devices. But he punctuates the monologue with the publican's ominous refrain, redolent of doomsday: "HURRY UP PLEASE ITS TIME."

The moral judgment suggested by this refrain is wasted on the speaker. The idea of accountability for one's life punctuates, but does not penetrate, the dreary uselessness of the lives depicted in the narration. As in the opulent scene preceding it, the moral insight is carried through the pub monologue by a sparse lyrical technique within a dramatic milieu. The key of deliverance from the horrifying sterility of both situations is seen in a union through purgation suggested by the Shakespearean allusion. "Those are pearls that were his eyes" indicates, in Ariel's song, that the king has suffered "a sea-change / Into something rich and strange." He has been purged by the tempest, and this purgation issues in a reconciliation between brothers and a union of two houses through the marriage of their children. Marriage is a symbol of union. Union is seen as salvation. In "A Game of Chess" marriage is the juxtaposition of spiritually polarized beings, each enclosed by isolated selfhood. It is a form of damnation.

In both parts of "A Game of Chess" Eliot signals the reader's perspective on the situations observed by means of lyric devices. We see this same technique operating in "The Fire Sermon," which is shot through with allusive lyrical segments of other poems carrying irony in their transference.

The first passage, depicting the banks of the Thames deserted after the summer season and the nymphs equally deserted by the "heirs of city directors," is punctuated by Spenser's lovely celebration of the marriage ceremony: "Sweet Thames, run softly, till I end my song." But the words from the "Prothalamion" only make one realize how much the ceremony of innocence is drowned in the lifeless rituals of these Thames celebrants. By means of this refrain Eliot punctuates his first verse paragraph in the traditional lyric manner of incremental repetition. The initial occurrence after the first four lines is less meaningful than the second, for the scene it terminates is simply one of an autumn landscape—desolate, but not unnaturally stagnant. We do not yet perceive the ominous meaning of "The wind / Crosses the brown land unheard," nor the significance of the minor refrain "The nymphs are departed." The second occurrence of Spenser's refrain closes a unit depicting the broken relationships. Thus the minor refrain about the nymphs takes on a dimension of greater specificity which adds in turn to the incremental nature of the refrain proper. The lines of repetition thus ring back upon themselves with increased meaning and give the measuring rod of evaluation on the scene depicted. The poet makes these slight lyrical touches work for him.

Eliot leavens the whole unit with a note of human passion by the insertion of the modified line from Psalm 137, wherein the exiled Hebrews refuse to sing the songs of Zion in a strange land: "By the waters of Babylon we sat down and wept. . . ." It is a psalm expressing abolute belonging and absolute fidelity to God and to a communal identity: "May I never speak again / if I forget you!" It is a strong contrast to the scene at hand. In substituting Leman for Babylon, moreover, Eliot underscores the contrast with irony. Babylon, after all, is a place of exile. One does not expect much from it. The associations of Leman, however, are ones of union—whether the word refers to friend, lover, or the League of Nations.

Eliot, by doubling and slightly adjusting the Spenserian refrain after the second unit capped by the psalm allusion, punctuates the whole passage and prepares for what is to follow. "Sweet Thames, run softly till I end my song, / Sweet Thames, run softly, for I speak not loud or long." One does not have to speak loud or long when he can manipulate his lyric material to serve as emotional and moral commentary and fulcrum. The passage gains economy and strength by tasteful and efficient use of this lyric refrain.

The shift that begins with the closing lines of the first verse paragraph hinges on the Marvell allusion: "But at my back in a cold blast I hear / The rattle of bones, and chuckle spread from ear to ear." The tone here is a far cry from "To His Coy Mistress," yet it is pointing to the same thing: the imminence of death. The passage that follows sustains the tone set by these lines, and a further modification of them brings the verse paragraph to a close that peters out in the "Red Wing" jingle about Mrs. Porter and her daughter. The unlovely passage ending in prostitution is infiltrated by lines from *The Tempest,* and closes with voices of the children singing in the cupola from Verlaine's *Parsifal.* Once more these bits of allusion stand against the wasteland milieu with provocative insistence.

After a sad reminder of Philomel and Tereus and a glimpse of Mr. Eugenid Eliot gives us the scene between the typist and the clerk. After rape and homosexual promiscuity, we have heterosexual activity with no union of person. The mechanical monotony of the meter reflects well the unfeeling ritual enacted by the two. The fact that Tiresias has "foresuffered all / Enacted on this same divan or bed" is Eliot's commentary on the dreary endlessness of human relations unredeemed by love. No grandeur is imparted by the allusion, and no contrast is implied. Tiresias suffers by the association, as did Cleopatra in "A Game of Chess."

Contrast is provided, however, by Eliot's parody of Goldsmith's lyric from *The Vicar of Wakefield.* In the original lyric, "When lovely woman stoops to folly / And finds too late that men betray," she has no way of eradicating her guilt and sorrow except death. The typist's reaction, "Well, now that's done: and I'm glad it's over," is far removed from this attitude. The somewhat maudlin double-standard morality of Goldsmith's poem is not what Eliot is suggesting by the allusion. The contrast serves to show the total lack of feeling on the part of the typist, the total lack of significance to what normally should be a fairly meaningful act. For Eliot the solution is another kind of death. The typist and the clerk each need to die to the unfeeling treadmill life they are leading. At the beginning of the episode the typist is referred to as "the human engine"; at the closing "She smoothes her hair with automatic hand, / And puts a record on the gramophone." What interrupts her routine is "a young man carbuncular" whose "vanity requires no response, / And makes a welcome of indifference." Such a desensitized life needs purging in order to restore it to vitality. As we have seen, this is not a passing problem in Eliot. It is his main concern to the end: the need of restoration for a world which "moves / In appetency, on its metalled ways" ("Burnt Norton" 3).

By means of another line from *The Tempest,* "This music crept by me upon the waters," Eliot makes a neat transition from the mechanized music of the typist's gramophone to "The pleasant whining of a mandoline" accompanying the clatter and chatter pouring from the public bar in Lower Thames Street. It is a scene of vitality and beauty,

where the walls
Of Magnus Martyr hold
Inexplicable splendour of Ionian white and gold.

The passage is rich with rime and onomatopoeia. Its free flow of rhythm throughout the whole unit, except for the penultimate verse, follows the base line of iambic pentamenter established by the initial quotation from Shakespeare. After the metrical constriction of the typist-clerk encounter, this richly rimed, open-vowelled, free-flowing rhythm is a relief that concurs with the subject matter. The final couplet, with its beautiful image of Magnus Martyr and open vowels, brings the scene to a close and prepares for the Elizabeth and Leicester episode that follows.

This lyric is swift with its irregularly placed rime in a basic two-stress line structure maintained throughout both stanzas except for the deviation in the middle three lines of the first:

Red sails
Wide
To leeward, swing on the heavy spar,

which fits, by its deviation, the image of swinging sails.

The first stanza sets the scene in modern Thames; the second shows Elizabeth and Leicester in their

. . . gilded shell
Red and gold
. . . .
Carried down stream.

Once again Eliot, by deliberate anachronism, splices together two pieces of time, thus equating them by association, and intimating the universality of human nature. The first stanza is full of the energy of modern commerce, but the Wagnerian refrain brings attention to the real ugliness of the river sweating oil and tar. In *Götterdämmerung* (3.1) the Rhine-maidens lament the beauty of the river, lost with the gold of the Nibelungs. At first it might seem that Eliot is thereby lamenting the lost beauty of the Elizabethan age. But here again he seems to equate and condemn by association.

The consistent dimeter rhythm of the second stanza briskly carries a beautiful picture of the royal barge beating downstream past white towers to the peal of bells. Yet this lovely setting, so suggestive of life, is presided over by Elizabeth and Leicester, whose idle flirtations recall a sterile love affair leading to betrayal and execution. The stanza is closed by the same Wagnerian refrain lamenting the loss of beauty and happiness—the beauty of the river, the happiness of the nymphs. In the opera the song of the Rhine-maidens, "Weialala leia," encloses the scene where they try to gain back the gold, first by flirting with Siegfried, then by trying to frighten him by predicting his doom in direct consequence of possessing the ring of gold. Both methods fail, and they return to the depths of the river singing their song. Eliot's insertion of this as a closing refrain to both river scenes is not promising.

The three Thames-daughters, who follow this lyric with their tales of lost innocence, parallel and contrast with the Rhine-maidens. They are a contrast because they are not mythical, preternatural beings, but lower class girls from resort towns. They are a parallel because, like the Rhine-maidens, they lament the loss of what they were responsible for guarding. With this loss goes their own happiness. The girls here are undone by the resort towns they have frequented. Each of the speakers shares with the others the sad story of her particular downfall—each narration, of course, is a recounting of a failure in love. Their tales are told with the resignation of hopelessness. The three vignettes are structured in a lyric discipline, the first two in fairly consistent four-stress lines of alternating rime. The metrics of the third disintegrate by inertia into irregularity while maintaining a fixed regularity of rime. The rimed words, moreover, form a remarkable condensation of the story:

> Sands . . . connect . . . nothing
> hands . . . expect . . . nothing.

Byron used this technique to great satiric effect. Whole sequences of *Beppo* and *Don Juan* are carried by the rime alone, which, lifted out, contains the narrative in skeleton.[1] It is not a practice associated with the lyric, yet

Eliot uses it here in a lyric section of his long poem. He manages to manipulate the technique for his own purposes in this lyric, and does it with truly fine skill to effect pathos unmixed with satire. Even the two preceding stanzas hint, in a less startling way, the narration in their rimes: "trees . . . Kew . . . knees . . . canoe"; "heart . . . event . . . new start . . . resent." This is a remarkably skillful and economical use of rime.

We saw in the preceding chapter how Eliot used rime for ironic purposes in "Prufrock" (pp. 13–14). Here he uses it to produce pathos. It would be hard to conceive a better way to achieve his ends with such economy, discipline, and delicacy of emotion. Without such lyric skill it would take many more verses to deliver the Thames-daughters of their sad narrations. The scenes are pinned down with a poignant particularity. The images are at once precise and universal. The last stanza emphasizes the sense of futility and emptiness by doubling the word "nothing" in the third verse, and by ending the poem on a monometer sixth line with a reiteration of "Nothing." The closing word is followed by the barest fragment, "la la," from the *Götterdämmerung* refrain which neatly links these three squalid love affairs with that of Elizabeth and Leicester, and shows a kinship between them through mutual sterility.

"The Fire Sermon" opens with deserted nymphs at the Thames, and closes with the Thames-daughters' tales of desertion. The closing lyric, unlike all the other episodes of futile love, is relieved by the mutual pity of the three narrators. In the coda which terminates part 3, there is a hint of hope in the fragments of St. Augustine's address to God: "O Lord thou pluckest me out of the burning." Because of Eliot's fragmentation we are not sure whether the protagonist's burning is Hell or Purgatory. That depends on the direction of his will. The significant point in this section of *The Waste Land,* as elsewhere, is that all the hints and intimations of real human value through love are effected by Eliot's careful use of lyrical techniques and allusions.

In "The Burial of the Dead" the protagonist, whose card is "the drowned Phoenician sailor," is warned to "Fear death by water" by Madame Sosostris, the famous clairvoyant who could not find the Hanged Man, and was not permitted to see what the one-eyed merchant carried on his back–both oblique references to the Crucifixion. Death by water has always been associated with baptism in Christian theology: the ritual burial of the spiritually dead into the death and Resurrection of Jesus. Though Madame Sosostris does not notice, her client sees or remembers: "Those are pearls that were his eyes. Look!" These references indicate a sea-change, a purgation of the drowned Phoenician sailor as he passes the stages of his age and youth.

"Death by Water" is an eight-line lyric in three stages, broken at the half-line twice, so that the first and last stanzas are each two and a half lines, while the middle one is three (two lines and two half-lines). This close division is not arbitrary. The verses are basically four-stress with heavy use of mid-caesura. In the two stanzaic divisions the caesura breaks both line and stanza, mirroring the dissolution which Phlebas is undergoing. That is the whole point of the lyric, and the metrics and rhythm exemplify it.

The subject could be horrifying (indeed it is in the unrevised manuscript),[2] yet the diction and tone-coloring give it another direction. The decorous antiphonal rhythm carries a sound heavy with sibilants and soft consonants. The diction is not selected for its possible charnel-house thrills, but resembles the purgation passage about the three white leopards in "Ash Wednesday." Considering the physical subject matter, it is a remarkable lyric. Eliot focuses on the mystery symbolized in the physical dissolution, and uses it as exemplum:

> Gentile or Jew
> O you who turn the wheel and look to windward,
> Consider Phlebas, who was once handsome and tall as you.

The drowned Phoenician sailor is to be an example, but not necessarily a horrible one. The overtones of baptism are unmistakable in view of the context of the lyric, and pave the way for the opening and message of "What the Thunder Said."

Before examining the last section, it is worth noticing the uniqueness of the "Death by Water" lyric within the structure of *The Waste Land.* It is self-contained, though its meaning depends on varied other references in the poem. No other part of *The Waste Land* consists of only one unit, and that a lyric. It occurs in the fourth part of the whole poem before the resolution or proposed solution is proffered in the fifth movement. In all these respects "Death by Water" is a foreshadowing of the fourth-part lyrics in *Four Quartets,* though its function within the total poem differs from the latter.

The inhabitants of the wasteland are like so many dead men: "I had not thought death had undone so many." In the first three movements Eliot shows various persons spiritually dead and unresponsive to any possible alternative: "The wind / Crosses the brown land unheard." Hints of a better life are lost. The land is arid; the people too are dried up. Both need rain, yet rain has been purposefully avoided throughout the poem. The opening lines voice a resentment that April should be "stirring / Dull roots with spring rain." In the first scene the speaker avoids rain:

> Summer surprised us, coming over the Starnbergersee
> With a shower of rain; we stopped in the colonnade,
> And went on in sunlight. . . .

In answer to the woman's question, "What shall we do tomorrow? / What shall we ever do?" the man in "A Game of Chess" replies: "The hot water at ten. / And if it rains, a closed car at four." Those who can, go south in the winter.

Madame Sosostris warns her client to "Fear death by water," but fails to see that the drowned Phoenician sailor does undergo a sea-change into something rich and strange: "(Those are pearls that were his eyes. Look!)." In part 4 we see this change as "A current under sea / Picked his bones in whispers." The death by water, so to be feared, seems less fearful, more mysterious than expected.

It is not surprising that in such a dry land the thunder holds the message of salvation. The thunder forewarns the coming of rain, and rain brings deliverance from a wasteland choking with aridity. When Eliot's thunder speaks words, those words proclaim the conditions for a possible rebirth through loving and responsible relationship: *Datta, Dayadhvam, Damyata* (Give, Sympathize, Control).

Throughout the poem Eliot has employed lyric devices to give a measure of emotion against which the emotionless can be judged. He inserts bits and fragments of allusion which momentarily short-circuit the condition of acedia. In "What the Thunder Said" his method is much more straightforward: the moments of grace, so to speak, have come and gone throughout the poem, and the wasteland remains in need of redemption from itself. Mysteriously, Phlebas exemplifies something to us which we are supposed to contemplate and apply to ourselves. Then comes the powerful opening of part 5:

> After the torchlight red on sweaty faces
> After the frosty silence in the gardens
> After the agony in stony places
> The shouting and the crying
> Prison and palace and reverberation
> Of thunder of spring over distant mountains
> He who was living is now dead
> We who were living are now dying
> With a little patience.

This verse paragraph is the only truly lyrical passage in "What the Thunder Said." It is a startling passage, breaking in upon us with its powerful music of solemn incantation. The triple anaphora of the opening lines, the heavy falling rhythms, the rime and assonance are fitting tools to carve out the strong Christic allusion. The passage is a remarkable condensation of the Passion narratives in the New Testament, particularly those of Matthew and Luke. But it is an equally remarkable recapitulation of some earlier scenes in *The Waste Land,* with its "frosty silence in the gardens" and its "agony in stony places." We are immediately reminded not only of the failure of the disciples during the agony in the garden at Gethsemane, but also of the silence of the lover in the hyacinth garden. We are reminded too of all the places of "stony rubbish" inhabited by wasteland characters. The double focus ties the two together with great economy and effectiveness, and implies that the land has a hero-rescuer who will restore it by his ordeal with death; that through identification the wasteland characters can share this deliverance by participating in this death. Like Phlebas they can be restored by "entering the whirlpool." With this passage the full meaning of "Death by Water" reveals itself. The baptism allusion of part 4 and the Passion allusion at the opening of part 5 are related in Christian scriptural theology. Perhaps the clearest exposition is in Paul's Epistle to the Romans.

> . . . Know ye not, that so many of us as were baptized into Jesus Christ were baptized into his death?
>
> Therefore we are buried with him by baptism into death: that like as Jesus Christ was raised up from the dead by the glory of the Father, even so we also should walk in newness of life.
>
> For if we have been planted together in the likeness of his death, we shall be also in the likeness of his resurrection. (Romans 6.3–5)

The persistent fragments from *The Tempest* strewn throughout the poem reinforce this interpretation, and make sense out of the playful irony of the paradox closing the passage:

> He who was living is now dead
> We who were living are now dying
> With a little patience.

This opening paragraph, therefore, is oriented toward resolution, not hopelessness. It is followed by a waterless journey through mountains of rock accompanied by hallucination and nightmare, but the journey leads to the Chapel Perilous, the ultimate place of ordeal, where the cock sings in a flash, not of betrayal but of illumination: "Then a damp gust / Bringing rain." It is indeed a quiet climax. From it emanates the message of the thunder: Give, Sympathize, Control. The message is veiled in a remote language, but is nonetheless valid. The words need translation just as the ideas they embody need translation into reality. Without hitting the reader over the head, the poem does lead to, or at least points to, a resolution.

Throughout *The Waste Land* the spiritually dead are prodded by moments of memory of a better life and desire for a better life. These hints and guesses are conveyed by means of lyrical techniques in a milieu of narration, dramatization, and exposition. It is a swift and efficient way to provide a norm against which to judge the quality of life depicted in the poem.

"THE HOLLOW MEN"

Eliot uses a different method entirely in "The Hollow Men." This is not surprising, for it is a very different poem from *The Waste Land.* Lyricism seems to take over completely as the hollow men virtually sing their way through all five movements. But the music here does not set up a contrast with the spiritual state of the speakers. Instead it embodies that state. It functions as a protective screen softening the speakers' perception of reality. The quiet music mesmerizes the sensibility. Here we have music as anodyne.

The hollow men are gathered on the beach of the tumid river waiting to cross over into "death's other Kingdom." They will not cross with direct eyes as do such lost violent souls as Mr. Kurtz and Guy Fawkes. They are like the nearly soulless whom Dante places in the vestibule of Hell: wretches who were never really alive, and therefore cannot truly die ("Questi sciaurati, che mai non fur vivi") (*Inferno* 3.64). Nameless and unremembered, they are gathered in the "starless air," rejected by Heaven and Hell alike. The hollow men are en route between "death's dream kingdom" and "death's other Kingdom," but we sense that they will never get there. They are dead men no matter where they are; death in one form or another is their kingdom. The hollow men keep their eyes averted. They ward off experience.

Eliot embodies this quality in his various structures. The short, two-stress basic line tends to disintegrate continually and grow slack, at times breaking down to one metrical foot, at others stretching out to four. The almost total lack of punctuation reinforces the idea of fragmentation and collapse. The rime is haphazard but plentiful, sometimes governing most of a verse paragraph, sometimes chiming only two words of a stanza, sometimes occurring internally. Frequently Eliot resorts to repeating words instead of riming. The effect produced is one of enervation. Nothing gets done. The hollow men are intent on avoiding a dreaded encounter:

> Let me be no nearer
> In death's dream kingdom
> Let me also wear
> Such deliberate disguises . . .
> Not that final meeting
> In the twilight kingdom.[3]

The encounter never occurs, the landscape is only half seen, and even that is fragmentary. The senses are confused in unhealthy synaesthesia:

> There, the eyes are
> Sunlight on a broken column
> There, is a tree swinging
> And voices are
> In the wind's singing
> More distant and more solemn
> Than a fading star.

Eliot's images are generalized and overwrought with biblical and classical allusions that lead the speakers nowhere, but provide a norm on which to assess their spiritual stupor.

In the last section Eliot moves out of this lovely, effete music into straight philosophical language which reiterates the problem of the hollow men. But philosophical formulation does not help them move. They remain like the people inside the Hell gate whom Dante describes as the woeful people who have lost the good of the intellect ("le genti dolorose / c'hanno perduto il ben dell'intelletto") (*Inferno* 3.17–18). Their philosophy is punctuated by abortive utterances from the end of the Lord's Prayer: "Thine is the Kingdom." The manner of the refrain technique used here is an organic representation of the philosophical statement of despair:

> Between the idea
> And the reality
> Between the motion
> And the act
> Falls the Shadow.

The capitalization, together with the refrain placement, neatly contrasts the Kingdom of God, "the perpetual star / Multifoliate rose," with the twilight kingdom, "death's dream kingdom" inhabited by the hollow men. Eliot's use of the refrain allusion here is reminiscent of that same technique in *The Waste Land.*

He sandwiches the whole last section within the nonsense lyrics of childhood games. The tone of these jingles is in shocking contrast to the Platonic utterance they enclose. Because of the intervening philosophy, moreover, the first jingle, "*Here we go round the prickly pear,*" retroactively takes on an ominous tone. The parts thus interact ironically. It would be hard to find a more suitable ironic commentary on these "nowhere men" with their shadow philosophy. They have indeed lost the good of the intellect, and can only go whimperingly around the prickly pear in endless futility. Throughout the first four movements Eliot's particular form of lyricism exemplifies the spiritual state of the hollow men. In the final section Eliot drops the lyric base and uses straight ratiocination. The lyrical elements act upon the philosophy in two important ways: the refrain from the Lord's Prayer, its utterance incomplete, shows the hopelessness of the hollow men's ideology; the beginning and ending turn upon the nonsense jingle shows the straight rationality to be no more than a running in circles.

The end of *The Waste Land* is ambiguous. The thunder has given the salvific message, but we are not sure whether the Fisher King is saved, or whether he is merely *aware* of salvation but too effete to make an act of the will. The submerged parts of the fragments he is shoring up hint at salvation, but the end is uncertain. There is no doubt about the hollow men. They are lost and hopeless. This poem is rock bottom in the Eliot scale. With the publication of "Ash Wednesday" we perceive a "struggle beyond hope and despair" as the protagonist mounts the saint's stair of purgation, relying all the while on the mysterious intercessory figure who has the power to make strong the fountains and make fresh the springs.

"ASH WEDNESDAY"

In "Ash Wednesday," as in *The Waste Land,* Eliot employs lyricism as an intensifier of reality and emotional awareness. As in "The Hollow Men," the lyricism is pervasive. Through the lyrical qualities of the verse Eliot conveys a sense of transcendent experience perceived as reality but not quite understood. In this respect the lyric quality of "Ash Wednesday" bears affinity to that used in *Four Quartets,* but structurally the usage is quite different in the two poems. In "Ash Wednesday" the lyric qualities spill over into the entire substance. There is no concentration of the material into a separate lyric that embodies the entire subject of the poem.

"Ash Wednesday" and the *Ariel Poems,* all published between 1927 and 1930, are Eliot's first outright religious poetry, and these poems reveal a theological position far removed from midwestern Unitarianism and New England Puritanism, the two forces that comprised Eliot's religious formation. The theology is that of Dante and John of the Cross. We have seen that Eliot as critic and as artist is one man. There is a continual correspondence evident in his work so that his poetry exemplifies his constantly reiterated opinions (cf. pp. 8-9). We see as early as 1920 some definite aesthetic judgments concerning Puritanism. In his essay on William Blake Eliot writes: "We may speculate, for amusement, whether it would not have been beneficial to the north of Europe generally, and to Britain in particular, to have had a more continuous religious history. . . ." He regrets specifically the loss of the old native deities and local divinities which the Italians, on their part, have managed to keep alive. "And perhaps our mythology was further impoverished by the divorce from Rome. Milton's celestial and infernal regions are large but insufficiently furnished apartments filled with heavy conversation; and one remarks about Puritan mythology its thinness" (*SE,* p. 279).

Writing on Andrew Marvell in 1921, Eliot notes that "Marvell's best verse is the product of European, that is to say Latin, culture (*SE,* p. 252). He praises Marvell for his wit: "It is in Propertius and Ovid. It is a quality of a sophisticated literature; a quality which expands in English literature just at the moment before the English mind altered; it is not a quality which we should expect Puritanism to encourage" (*SE,* p. 255-56). In his notorious bout with Milton in 1936, Eliot attacks not just the poetics but the theology as well: "So far as I perceive anything, it is a glimpse of a theology that I find in large part repellent, expressed through a mythology which would have better been left in the Book of *Genesis,* upon which Milton has not improved" (*PP,* p. 163).

None of these examples of Eliot's anti-Puritanism is related to his religious conversion. They are aesthetically oriented comments, but show a corresponding theological bias which is exemplified in the religious poems of the late twenties, culminating in "Ash Wednesday" and "Marina," 1930.

The idea of purgation has a long history, and runs like a thread through the poems of Eliot. In his essay entitled "Dante" (1929) he remarks that purgation is difficult, for it involves too much "that is strange to the modern mind" (*SE,* p. 212). The popularity of the *Inferno* over the *Purgatorio* attests to this insight. It is paralleled, in Eliot's case, by the popularity of *The Waste Land* and "The Hollow Men" over that of "Ash Wednesday." Commenting on the difference between the suffering of damnation and that of purgation, Eliot remarks: ". . . we see clearly how the flame of purgatory differs from that of hell. In hell, the torment issues from the very nature of the damned themselves, expresses their essence; they writhe in torment of their own perpetually perverted nature. In purgatory the torment of flame is deliberately and consciously accepted by the penitent." (*SE,* pp. 216-17)

One of the most poignant modern artistic expressions of this attitude, the deliberate desire for purgation as an act of the will, is in John Henry Newman's *The Dream of Gerontius,* from which Eliot may have gotten his title for "Gerontion." The "old man," confused after death by the face-to-face encounter with the beauty and goodness of God, realizes he cannot stand the beatific vision because of his own sinfulness. His response is:

Take me away, take me away, and in the lowest deep
There let me be,
And there in hope the long night-watches keep,
Told out for me.
There, motionless and happy in my pain,
Lone, not forlorn
There will I sing my sad perpetual strain
Until the morn.
There will I sing and soothe my stricken breast,
Which ne'er can cease
To throb, and pine, and languish, till possest
Of its Sole Peace.[4]

The Dantesque passage which seems most to affect Eliot on this score recounts Arnaut Daniel's speech to Dante in the *Purgatorio:*

"Ieu sui Arnaut, que plor e vau cantan;
consiros vei la passada folor,
e vei jausen lo joi qu'esper, denan.
Ara vos prec, per aquella valor
que vos guida al som de l'escalina,
sovegna vos a temps de ma dolor!"
Poi s'ascose nel foco che li affina.
(26.142–48)

"I am Arnaut, who weeps and goes singing. I see in grief past follies, and see in joy the day I hope for before me. And so I pray you, by that virtue which guides you to the summit of the stair, be mindful, in time, of my pain." Then he hid himself in that fire which refines them.

Eliot uses "Ara vos prec" as the title of the English edition of *Poems, 1920,* which opens with "Gerontion." He uses the last line of the passage as one of the fragments which the Fisher King is shoring up against his ruins in *The Waste Land.* "Sovegna vos" is addressed to the intercessory lady in part 4 of "Ash Wednesday." In assessing these lines in his essay on Dante (*SE,* p. 217), Eliot refers to them as "superb verses." He is surely moved by the passage, and its influence is pervasive in Eliot.

But this is difficult material, and in "Ash Wednesday" Eliot was still too close to the experience of religious conversion to condense it into a tightly wrought precision of expression as he will later do in the *Four Quartets* lyrics. Eliot is not alone in the difficulty he undergoes in trying to communicate the experience of purgation. In his "Prologue" to *The Ascent of*

Mount Carmel, St. John of the Cross begins by cautioning his reader:

> A deeper enlightenment and wider experience than mine is necessary to explain the dark night through which a soul journeys toward that divine light of perfect union with God which is achieved, insofar as possible in this life, through love. The darkness and trials, spiritual and temporal, that fortunate souls ordinarily encounter on their way to the high state of perfection are so numerous and profound that human science cannot understand them adequately; nor does experience of them equip one to explain them. He who suffers them will know what this experience is like, but he will find himself unable to describe it.[5]

The way John of the Cross does describe it is with the ecstatic joy of his poetry, where he tries to capture that experience which he then translates into prose commentary. It is an experience of *no sabiendo,* of unknowing. The kinship is striking between John's expression and that of the fourteenth-century English mystic who described the purgative state in *The Cloud of Unknowing:*

> When you first begin, you find only darkness, and as it were a cloud of unknowing. You don't know what this means except that in your will you feel a simple steadfast intention reaching out towards God. Do what you will, this darkness and this cloud remain between you and God, and stop you . . . from seeing him in the clear light of rational understanding. . . . Reconcile yourself to wait in this darkness as long as is necessary. . . . For if you are to feel him or to see him in this life, it must always be in this cloud, in this darkness.[6]

I cite these passages at length because these classics show the same characteristics. Whether it be the thirteenth-century Tuscan poet, or the fourteenth-century English parson, or the sixteenth-century Spanish mystic, the tradition of the purgative state shows a consistent combination of qualities: first, a willing acceptance of suffering because it will cleanse the person from the sin that has caused isolation from God and neighbor; second, a joyful resignation to the suffering because of the absolute, unshakable hope that it will bring about the desired end: thus Arnaut's singing and John of the Cross's rhapsodizing. Eliot's music is not out of place in such a tradition.

The music of "Ash Wednesday" is delicate and insistent, communicating the mystery and peace of the speaker in the purgatorial state. It is the right medium for conveying the poet's experience at this time. Speaking of Dante, Eliot says "that genuine poetry can communicate before it is understood (*SE,* p. 200). He notes in Dante "a poetic as distinguished from an *intellectual* lucidity" (p. 201). Although Eliot is writing in his native tongue, he is speaking from a spiritual state whose language is tantamount to a foreign tongue for the large part of his audience. It is the language of mysticism with a long history, which the Anglo-Catholic Eliot has inherited as spiritual legacy through Rome.[7] The language is unfamiliar to the modern reader and makes demands. Yet the music is immediately apprehensible though the meaning is at first elusive.

The poem is predominantly in delicate falling rhythm, further emphasized by the many feminine rimes. Rime spills over from end rime to internal and even to the merely visual ("dolour-colour"). Eliot seems careless about the patterning of sound. The sound-structure gets its total effect by its pervasiveness. The lyricism, however, has a powerful concentration in two outstanding devices: the liturgical refrains which signal the direction the speaker is taking, so that the whole of "Ash Wednesday" reveals itself as a spiritual journey; and the fine distillation of the paradox of purgation in the Irish litany section of part 2. We need to examine each section briefly to see how the refrain works within the total movement of the poem. The litany will be examined in its place in part 2.

The rhythm of part 1 is dominated by the anaphoric use of the opening lines of Cavalcanti's ballata, "Perch' io non spero," written in exile from Tuscany. The allusion establishes the analogue of spiritual exile, the weaning of the speaker from the familiar world of ordinary pursuits, "Desiring this man's gift and that man's scope." This slight alteration of Shakespeare's Sonnet 29 from "art" to "gift" places the exile in a more universal, not merely a literary state of deprivation. The tone of part 1 is one of calm, unpretentious self-assessment and desire to forget "These matters that with myself I too much discuss / Too much explain." The prayer of part 1 is that of resignation: "Teach us to care and not to care / Teach us to sit still." But the speaker does not expect his prayer to be answered on his own merit. He turns to the end of the *Ave Maria* and addresses the Virgin: "Pray for us sinners now and at the hour of our death / Pray for us now and at the hour of our death."

Part 1 closes with a prayer to Mary. Part 2 opens with an address to a lady who presides over the protagonist's dissembling by the three white leopards under a juniper tree in the desert. As in "Death by Water" the tone here is serene and shows a subdued joy, contrary to what one would expect from the subject matter. From the marrow of his scattered dry bones comes the reason for the joy:

> Because of the goodness of this Lady
> And because of her loveliness, and because
> She honors the Virgin in meditation,
> We shine with brightness.

The threefold use of "because" is markedly different from the self-conscious, somewhat sententious anaphora at the opening of part 1. The focus of the speaker is no longer on himself, but on the intercessory figure by whose goodness his suffering is turned into purgation. The lady in the white gown is like Dante's Matilda who inhabits the Earthly Paradise at the summit of the Mount of Purgatory. She is the human race restored to radical innocence, and thus to Eden. Once the soul has climbed the purgatorial mountain, it has been purged of all its sins. Only the memory of sin remains. This needs to be left behind before passing into Paradise. Only after Matilda has submerged Dante in the waters of Lethe is he ready for the smile of Beatrice, the smile of Divine Love.

The paradoxical prayer to the "Lady of silences" which follows manifests the traditional Christian attitude toward Mary, who is both *Mater dolorosa* and *Mater beatissima* in the early litanies. Here she is "Torn and most whole," "Exhausted and life-giving." The lyrical tightness of the passage perfectly embodies in its structural dualities the paradox addressed. The rare dactylic dimeter rhythms further reflect the duality of idea. This metrical line is too short to sustain rime without being singsong, but there is much internal chiming and playing with chiasmic structure–"Speech without word and / Word of no speech"–which enhance significantly the idea of duality in purgation.

By the opening reference to the juniper tree, the speaker in part 2 is associated with the spiritual struggle of Elijah in the desert (1 Kings 19). At the end, after the litany, we find the bones still singing under the juniper tree, "scattered and shining," forgetting themselves as they had prayed in part 1. Part 2 ends with a glimpse of the promised land: "This is the land. We have our inheritance." The ambiguity here echoes that of the "Lady of silences" lyric which immediately precedes it. "This" refers to the land of the bones, but by implication points to the inheritance that comes from joyful acceptance of the desert–"The desert in the garden the garden in the desert" referred to in part 5 and underscored by the use of chiasmus.

The immediate inheritance of the soul bent upon purgation is the saint's stair of part 3. At the climax of this section the protagonist has reached the state prayed for in part 1's "Teach us to sit still." By the end he comes to a "strength beyond hope and despair / Climbing the third stair." The section is punctuated by the prayer of the centurion (Luke 7.6–7) as used in the Mass:

> Lord, I am not worthy
> Lord, I am not worthy
> but speak the word only.

Liturgically the line is recited immediately before the Holy Communion, when the participant receives the body and blood of Christ, the Word of God. Characteristically Eliot aborts his quoted material so as to leave out what follows: "Lord, I am not worthy that Thou shouldst enter under my roof; speak only the word and my soul shall be healed." By liturgical implication, then, what will follow upon the speaking of the word is the healing of the soul's sickness.

Part 1 ends with the prayer from the *Ave Maria:* "Pray for us now and at the hour of our death." The hour of death takes shape with the dissembling of the bones in part 2. When active spiritual struggle is manifested in the stair sequence of part 3, the speaker prays the communion prayer of the Mass. Just as Dante emerges from the Mount of Purgatory into the Earthly Paradise where all memory of past sin is wiped out and he is given joy by the dream vision of the Griffon and the smile of Beatrice, so now in part 4 Eliot presents a dream vision of an intercessory figure "Going in white and blue, in Mary's colour." The prayer of Arnaut, "Sovegna vos," is evoked merely by the sight of her. Her mysterious power of presence can restore the desert: "Who then made strong the fountains and made fresh the springs / Made cool the dry rock and made firm the sand." Renewal follows immediately upon the prayer to this lady. The years "between sleeping and waking" are borne away, and

> The new years walk, restoring
> Through a bright cloud of tears, the years, restoring
> With a new verse the ancient rhyme. Redeem
> The time. Redeem
> The unread vision in the higher dream
> While jewelled unicorns draw by the gilded hearse.

The garden god of part 3 is powerless to lure the protagonist away from his purgative way. The dream is, like Dante's Griffon, "The token of the word unheard, unspoken." It remains still for that word to be spoken. The movement ends with the fragment from the end of the *Salve Regina:* "And after this our exile." As with all of Eliot's fragments, the segment unheard is full of import. The line of the prayer continues with ". . . show unto us the blessed fruit of thy womb, Jesus."

This unvoiced prayer is answered in a partial revelation of the Word which follows in part 5. A glimpse of the Word emerges out of the punning meditation on the word borrowed from Lancelot Andrewes:

> Still is the unspoken word, the Word unheard,
> The Word without a word, the Word within
> The world and for the world.

It is not a total vision, but seen darkly as in the "Prologue" of St. John's Gospel:

> And the light shone in darkness and
> Against the Word the unstilled world still whirled
> About the center of the silent Word.

The image puts the light at the center of the silent Word. The world is redeemed at the core and needs to wait for the reverberations of the Word to move outward. After this glimpse of the Word at the center of reality, comes the refrain: "O my people, what have I done unto thee." This sad line is spoken by God to his people in the Reproaches of the Good Friday liturgy:

> Popule meus, quid feci tibi?
> aut in quo contristavite?
> responde mihi.
>
> Quia eduxi te de terra Aegypti:
> parasti crucem Salvatori tuo.
> (Roman Missal)

My people, what have I done to thee, or in what have I grieved thee? Answer me. Because I led thee out of the land of Egypt, thou hast prepared a cross for thy Savior.

It is significant that these reproaches belong to the ancient ritual of a public penance. They occur in the liturgy during the solemn veneration of the cross by the people—a ritual sign of repentance for sin and a sign of their purgation. Eliot introduces the first refrain following the first paragraph where the speaker, through contemplation, gets a fleeting insight into the Word of God. The refrain recurs after the next two-paragraph unit, the first of which loses sight of the word (and by implication, the Word) in the noisy avoidance of life: "No place of grace for those who avoid the face / No time to rejoice for those who walk among the noise and deny the voice." But the paragraph following this loss addresses the problem of restoration to the intercessory figure:

> . . . Will the veiled sister pray
> For children at the gate
> Who will not go away and cannot pray:
> Pray for those who chose and oppose.

The reproach follows once again, but the presence of "the veiled sister," who prays for "those who walk in darkness," gives hope that her intercessory power will prevail, and she will dissipate the darkness here as she relieved the drought in the preceding section.

The last paragraph continues the struggle of those who "are terrified and cannot surrender / . . . In the last desert between the last blue rocks." The struggle is nearing the end. It is the "last desert," after all, and the rocks are "Mary's colour"–a reminder that the struggle is not without help. Part 4 ended with the prayer, "And after this our exile [show unto us the blessed fruit of thy womb, Jesus]." In part 5 a reproachful God answers, but a reproach is better than a refusal to respond. And in the end the withered appleseed is spit out, the remnant of the original sin. The last desert is perceived as "The desert in the garden the garden in the desert." The chiasmic structure, significantly unpunctuated, links Eden lost and Eden restored in a powerful grammatical integration. The refrain closing the movement is aborted to "O my people." It can be interpreted, not as reproach, but as a smile of divine love following complete purgation.

The fact that the poem does not end with part 5 demonstrates that for the protagonist there is still the working out of purgation as an inhabitant of earth. Dante too had to return and resume his earthly life after the high dream. The mystical experience is a foreshadowing, a taste of future bliss, but the years still bring their temptations and wavering response. This is the subject of the sixth and final part. The circular structure of "Ash Wednesday" is evident in the anaphoric alteration of part 1: "Although I do not hope to turn again. . . ." The speaker admits he is beset by renewed desire for what has already been relinquished. In "The Dry Salvages" Eliot will describe these things as ". . . what was believed in as the most reliable– / And therefore the fittest for renunciation" ("The Dry Salvages" 2). After his vision the protagonist is back once more "In this brief transit where the dreams cross / The dreamcrossed twilight between birth and dying"; and all that is "fittest for renunciation" comes back in some of the most lyrically beautiful lines of poetry written in our century. Significantly, the passage begins with the ritual formula for the confession of sins:

> (Bless me father) though I do not wish to wish these things
> From the wide window towards the granite shore
> The white sails still fly seaward, seaward flying
> Unbroken wings
>
> And the lost heart stiffens and rejoices
> In the lost lilac and the lost sea voices
> And the weak spirit quickens to rebel

For the bent golden-rod and the lost sea smell
Quickens to recover
The cry of quail and whirling plover
And the blind eye creates
The empty forms between the ivory gates
And smell renews the salt savor of the sandy earth.

This points indeed beyond the mere renunciation of sin. It is of the tradition of John of the Cross, Juliana of Norwich, *The Cloud of Unknowing.* A quotation from the last illustrates the kinship:

So pay great attention to this marvellous work of grace within your soul. It is always a sudden impulse and comes without warning, springing up to God like some spark from the fire. An incredible number of such impulses arise in one brief hour in the soul who has a will to this work! In one such flash the soul may completely forget the created world outside. Yet almost as quickly it may relapse back to thoughts and memories of things done and undone—all because of our fallen nature. And as fast again it may rekindle. (p. 57).

Every page of John of the Cross reflects the same insight. In part 6 it is not the idyllic fantasy world of the garden god which returns to disrupt the protagonist's peace, but rather the good things of the real world—the lost Eden which the speaker does not feel worthy of repossessing. The power of their beauty and the accompanying sense of loss are intensified by the loveliness of the verse: the hidden discipline under the free-flowing lines; the beauty of the rimes, assonance, and alliteration; the piercing familiarity of the images. One is reminded of the dream vision of part 4, ". . . restoring / Through a bright cloud of tears, the years." The speaker is still in "the time of tension between dying and birth," but he has gone beyond the three white leopards and the fiddles and the flutes to "The place of solitude" where the yew of mortality and the yew of immortality respond to each other.

Part 6 concludes with a prayer to the Virgin who incorporates all the other intercessory figures: "Blessed sister, holy mother, spirit of the fountain, spirit of the garden." The prayer is for integrity: "Suffer us not to mock ourselves with falsehood." The prayer in part 1 is reiterated—"Teach us to care and not to care / Teach us to sit still"—amid the blue rocks of the desert, at peace because united with the will of God: "Our peace in His will." The Marian image expands from garden and fountain to "spirit of the river, spirit of the sea." Garden and fountain are images of Paradise. River and sea are images of earthly life, of passage. In this life the speaker ends his prayer with a desire not to be separated from God. He ends with the liturgical coda, "And let my cry come unto thee." The blank between the coda and the last line can be filled, again, with what Eliot has left out—the direct address to God: "O Lord, hear my prayer."

The two direct addresses to God concluding parts 3 and 6 form a perfect balance. Both come after a struggle with earthly delights. In part 3 the prayer before Communion ("O Lord, I am not worthy") is followed immediately in part 4 by communion, through insight, with the Word. The closing of part 6 comes from the closing of each of the nine canonical hours of the Divine Office, the *Opus Dei.* Liturgically the hours of the Office carry over the action of the Mass through the entire day and night; the Mass carries the redemptive act of Christ through diurnal space and time. Symbolically, therefore, the Mass and Office are continual and cyclic actions of incremental renewal until the end of the individual's life and the end of time itself. Eliot's familiarity with the Mass and the Divine Office is manifest in "Ash Wednesday."

The codas of parts 1 and 4 are from the *Ave Maria* and the *Salve Regina* respectively, both Marian lyrics: the first, an embellishment on Luke's Annunciation narrative which places Mary in the role of intercessor for the human race; the second, the lyric which closes compline, the last hour of the Divine Office, for the last season of the liturgical year. The two Marian codas symbolically span the salvation event from the Annunication of Christ to the end of the life of each individual. Eliot's use of fragments is, therefore, undoubtedly significant. Part 2 has no coda, but contains the lyrical Irish litany representing the duality of paradox in its contemplation of Mary. Only in part 5 does God speak, and it is in the form of a reiterated refrain marking a spiritual progression or evolution in the one addressed.. It is incremental, like most good refrains.

Eliot's use of sources in "Ash Wednesday" is amazing. His lyrical use of the ancient Christian liturgy gives shape and direction to what appears to be a dreamy meditation. The Dantesque material is couched in careful metrical and grammatical paradigms to telescope and encapsule the whole last sequence of the *Purgatorio.*

The problem is that one needs to be familiar with the Christian liturgy, the aesthetics of which embody its own meaning. Otherwise one cannot get the full richness of Eliot's method of allusion, or even more than the bare bones of what he is saying in "Ash Wednesday." This is a decided drawback, and Eliot's audience is limited by it. The situation is ironic because Eliot is drawing on a long tradition, not inventing one of his own. In a 1920 essay he notes a certain formlessness that marked William Blake's longer poems because he had to invent his own philosophy as well as poetry; whereas Dante, in borrowing a theory of the soul, was able to give form to his poetic presentation of that theory (*SE,* p. 278). Eliot, by using the theory of Dante and mystical theology and the aesthetics of liturgical prayer, is still up against the problem of obscurity discussed in the preceding chapter. Here the problem is compounded because the lyrical use of coda and refrain, which gives form to the meaning and clinches the interpretation, is from a source obscure to many. The beauty of the more diffuse and pervasive lyricism of "Ash Wednesday" is itself moving, but moving in what direction? There is danger of confusing it with the organically effete aesthetics of the hollow men inside the Hell gate. Yet the river to be crossed is Acheron on the one hand, and Lethe on the other. The terminal point of "The Hollow Men" is the damnation of isolation; that of "Ash Wednesday" is communion with God through purgation.

To state this problem of obscurity is not to devalue Eliot's craftsmanlike use of his sources. The reason for his obscurity is a lack of common coin between the religious poet and many modern readers. Actually it would be hard to find more useful and felicitous tools than those Eliot employs in this poem for shaping what could otherwise be vague and amorphous experience. It is organic form at its most original. To place the highly personal state of religious conversion in a universal frame, Eliot uses the best of a tradition. To Eliot it would be the most human way to approach the task: "Man is man because he can recognize supernatural realities, not because he can invent them."[8]

In his long poems Eliot uses lyric matter to intensify, contrast, enrich by allusion, give shape to difficult subject matter. For different reasons some of the poetry remains obscure. In all cases the lyricism itself helps elucidate. This is true even of "Ash Wednesday," given knowledge of his sources on the part of the reader. As he progresses from *The Waste Land* to "Ash Wednesday," he relies more and more on lyricism to convey emotion. But nowhere do we find a precedent for the particular function of the lyrics in *Four Quartets.*

His clarity, moreover, increases in the quartets, where Eliot manages to give expression to his religious convictions by using images less esoteric than those so far examined. The cloud of obscurity is dissipated. Eliot himself noted the quality of simplicity as the hallmark of *Four Quartets.* In an interview with Donald Hall in 1959, Eliot comments: "I see the later *Quartets* as being much simpler and easier to understand than *The Waste Land* and 'Ash Wednesday.' Sometimes the thing I'm trying to say, the subject matter, may be difficult, but it seems to me that I'm saying it in a simple way."[9] He attributes this simplicity to experience and maturity, not to a totally different view of life:

I think that in the early poems it was a question of not being able to—of having more to say than one knew how to say, and having something one wanted to put into words and rhythm which one didn't have the command of words and rhythm to put in a way immediately apprehensible.[10]

In saying this, Eliot is once again confronting, but with less tolerance than in *The Use of Poetry,* the problem of obscurity which has been a serious barrier to communication, and has both repelled and attracted many readers. He surely gives his early obscurity a forthright appraisal:

That type of obscurity comes when the poet is still at the stage of learning how to use language. You have to say the thing the difficult way. The only alternative is not saying it at all, at that stage. By the time of the *Four Quartets,* I couldn't have written in the style of *The Waste Land.* In *The Waste Land,* I wasn't even bothering whether I understood what I was saying.[11]

Eliot is very definitely bothering about the communication of meaning in *Four Quartets,* which he considers his best work, one on which his reputation would stand or fall.[12]

The successful combination of difficult subject matter and simplicity of exposition is certainly the fruit of experience. *Murder in the Cathedral* surely helped, and Eliot has noted the lesson of clarity which writing for the stage teaches a poet.[13] But it is also a continued attention to the lyric in criticism and in practice that accounts for the enormous success of the fourth-section lyrics in *Four Quartets.* Before considering their function within the architecture of the quartets, a marvel of "concentration without elimination," it would be useful to note their technical brilliance as individual, self-contained lyrics. Only after that assessment is made can one appreciate their place in the larger work, and perceive a new use for lyric verse which Eliot devises for his last substantial poetic work.

CHAPTER FOUR

AN APPRAISAL OF THE LYRIC MOVEMENTS IN *FOUR QUARTETS*

The lyrics of *Four Quartets* are marked by similarity as well as difference. In each there is a notable discipline of rhythm more or less relaxed or taut as the demands of the meaning structure dictate. Rhythm thus moves in a wide arc between the incantatory and the prosaic. No matter how closely the meter approaches the measured discipline of musical regularity, it never moves away from the ambient of the common idiom of spoken language. The same principle informs Eliot's style. His diction, for example, is never a liberation from common speech but a continual departure from and approximation of the spoken idiom. The demands of good prose act as a fulcrum for Eliot's poetic practice. He exploits grammatical structure for purposes of cadence, but the music produced is always an echo or implementation of the thought pattern. In Eliot's criticism fitness is invariably the norm for evaluation: fitness of parts to the whole structure, and fitness of techniques to meanings. He has followed his own principle so closely that it is difficult to determine in his practice whether the meaning inheres in the structure, or whether the structure mirrors the meaning.

Part of the investigation concerns the analysis of Eliot's rhythm. In determining the stress pattern of the lyrics, a recording of the poet's reading of *Four Quartets* was used. Since the whole nature of this study is based on Eliot's critical practice, the author's recording could not be ignored as an indication of his rhythms. Eliot himself sees this as the one value of such a recording:

> What the recording of a poem by its author can and should preserve, is the way that poem sounded to the author when he had finished it. The disposition of lines on a page, the punctuation . . . can never give an exact notation of the author's metric. The chief value of the author's record, then, is as a guide to the rhythms.[1]

The fourth-section lyrics will be studied in a sequence different from their arrangement by order of composition in *Four Quartets.*[2] Because of the traditional emphasis on musical regularity in lyric form, it is less problematic to investigate the two most regular lyrics before the others. Of these "East Coker" 4 is studied first since, because of its greater length and complexity, some of the theory brought to bear in its analysis can be conveniently referred to in the subsequent investigations. "Little Gidding" 4 follows because, in its similarity to the preceding lyric both in metrics and theme, it lends itself to a comparative study with "East Coker" 4. Moving out from the norm of regularity, "Burnt Norton" 4 follows with a pattern less evident than those of the two preceding lyrics. "The Dry Salvages" 4 comes last as the lyric most approaching free verse and farthest removed from the conventional disciplines of metric.

"EAST COKER" 4

The wounded surgeon plies the steel
That questions the distempered part;
Beneath the bleeding hands we feel
The sharp compassion of the healer's art
Resolving the enigma of the fever chart.

Our only health is the disease
If we obey the dying nurse
Whose constant care is not to please
But to remind of our, and Adam's curse,
And that, to be restored, our sickness must grow worse.

The whole earth is our hospital
Endowed by the ruined millionaire,
Wherein, if we do well, we shall
Die of the absolute paternal care
That will not leave us, but prevents us everywhere.

The chill ascends from feet to knees,
The fever sings in mental wires.
If to be warmed, then I must freeze
And quake in frigid purgatorial fires
Of which the flame is roses, and the smoke is briars.

The dripping blood our only drink
The bloody flesh our only food:
In spite of which we like to think
That we are sound, substantial flesh and blood—
Again, in spite of that, we call this Friday good.

The fourth section of "East Coker" is a passion lyric presenting the mystery of redemption through purgation. The Christian paradox of reaching wholeness through negation is set forth in a series of enigmatic sentences which reach their climax with the last word of the lyric. The theme is specifically religious, and apropos of the problem of writing what he calls devotional poetry, Eliot has much to say in his criticism. In commenting on Samuel Johnson's lack of appreciation for the seventeenth-century religious lyrics, Eliot notes that a general dulling of religious sensibility in the eighteenth century accounts for this.[3] He undoubtedly sees something analogous to this problem of communication in his own time, for a year after making his remark about the eighteenth-century religious sensibility he notes that the trouble with the modern age is not just the inability to believe certain things about God and man, but also the inability to *feel* toward God and man. He places great significance on the sensibility as such. A belief no longer believed can still be understood, "but when religious feelin disappears, the words in which men have struggled to express it become meaningless."[4] In the "East Coker" lyric Eliot has very definitely worked toward a communication of both thought and feeling. As he had said earlier, the poet should express the "emotional equivalent of thought";[5] he should aim for a "direct sensuous apprehension, or a recreation of thought into feeling."[6] This principle is one which Eliot has continually reiterated. Twenty years after making the statement just cited, he can reaffirm in his ex cathedra manner: "The first condition of right thought is right sensation.' In the "East Coker" lyric it is especially necessary for the poet to recreate this thought into feeling because the subject matter is particularly intractable

Eliot has said that purgation is a more difficult subject to render poeticall than either damnation or blessedness, which are more exciting and thereby more acceptable as poetic material.[8] He is displeased with poets who have worked in this material, yet have not done justice to its full significance. In 1940, for example, he expressed puzzlement with Yeats for rendering Purgatory without purgation.[9] And four years earlier Eliot had written: "I should not enjoy the prospect of abolishing suffering without at the same time perfecting human nature."[10] The lyric under question deals specificall with the perfection of human nature through redemptive suffering and there fore makes special technical demands on the poet before it can be rendered into something sensuously apprehended.

Eliot has used his technical apparatus to underscore the meaning. The two are so well integrated that "something results in which medium and material, form and content, are indistinguishable." They "are interesting as one thing, not as two."[11] This kind of fusion is another desideratum to which Eliot as critic returns continually and consistently. Almost thirty years after he made the foregoing remarks in an introduction to the *Selected*

Poems of Ezra Pound, he confirms his earlier position: "The notion of appreciation of form without content, or of content ignoring form is an illusion." Ignorance of one results in failure to appreciate or grasp the other.[12] One finds remarkable fitness of both style and sound structure to the subject matter of "East Coker" 4.

Eliot identifies style with "vocabulary, syntax, and order of thought."[13] In regard to each of these he has much to say throughout his body of critical writings. Eliot's norms for style can best perhaps be defined negatively in contrast to what qualities of style should be avoided. Of all the possible faults of style, Eliot seems to be particularly aware of certain ones: "The tumultuous outcry of adjectives, the headstrong rush of undisciplined sentences, are the index to the impatience and perhaps laziness of a disorderly mind."[14] The parallelism in the two foregoing statements of Eliot made one year apart is noteworthy. In one he arbitrarily selects those constituents of style which correspond exactly to his prior delineation of what he considered the worst faults against style. Taken together, the two statements constitute a neat scheme of stylistic elements paired off against their relative excesses:

Vocabulary	"The tumultuous outcry of adjectives."
Syntax	"The headstrong rush of undisciplined sentences.
Order of thought	"The impatience and . . . laziness of a disorderly mind."

An examination of "East Coker" 4 in terms of vocabulary, syntax, and order of thought will show a usage quite contrary to the faults associated with each of the three selected stylistic elements.

Eliot's sparse use of adjectives in the lyric is immediately noticeable. In 177 words there are only 25 attributive adjectives, and 8 of these ("our" used twice, "only" used three times, "constant," "absolute," "whole") are limiting rather than descriptive. Of those which perform any kind of descriptive function, 6 ("wounded," "distempered," "bleeding," "dying," "ruined," "dripping") are in verbal form, while 6 ("fever," "paternal," "mental," "purgatorial," "bloody," "substantial") are near substantives. Two of the modifying words ("healer's" and "Adam's") are only nominal adjectives. Only three ("sharp," "frigid," "sound") are pure adjectival forms. Sparseness is not the only quality noticeable in Eliot's use of adjectives. A particularly deft craftsmanship is evident in his handling of the last word of the lyric–the one adjective in the poem not grammatically placed in the usual attributive position before the substantive. "Good" in the last line is an objective complement, a rather unusual grammatical construction. Especially here, constituting as it does a reversal of a very familiar phrase, "Good Friday," the adjective calls attention to itself. The overtones of the word are intensified by the mode of inversion. Yet another piece of underscoring goes on naturally here; one must accent the objective complement in English whenever it is used. Staying within the strict grammatical limitations of the adjectival form, Eliot exploits word order to achieve a coincidence of emphasis in meter and meaning.

Besides the sparse use of adjectives there are other features of diction worth noticing. Though Eliot has said that poetry and language are inter-determining, and that the poet must take as his material his own language as spoken around him; yet he can to some extent preserve or restore the beauty of the language.[15] He takes strong exception to Valéry's complaint of semantic exhaustion in Europe: "My language is finished for me when I have come to the end of my resources, in endeavoring to extend and develop that language. . . . Every language, to retain its vitality, must perpetually depart and return upon itself; but without the departure there is no return, and the returning is as important as the arrival."[16] It seems that this is exactly what Eliot is doing in "East Coker" 4, which so much resembles the metaphysical lyric. He is exploiting the semantic fluidity of the English of an earlier period. If Eliot can complain that for twenty years modern poetry has been searching unsuccessfully for a modern idiom,[17] he himself seems to search for it in "an easy commerce of the old and the new." To speak of fe charts, wires, endowed hospitals, and ruined millionaries is certainly to place the poem in a contemporary frame of reference. Yet in checking the *OED* for the literary history of some of Eliot's words ("ply," "question," "distempered," "prevent," "substantial"), one finds how heavily he leans toward earlier usages. There is no problem about the meanings of these words, which are easily determined by their context in the poem. Yet it is surprising to find how frequently the usage obviously determined by the context is labelled "archaic," "obsolete," or "rare" in the *OED.*[18] By a formal association with an earlier type of lyric, the poet has made a simultaneous association with an earlier diction, resurrecting usages no longer common and placing them in a context that precludes any possibility of confusion. Richness, not imprecision, of meaning is gained in the process. There is no doubt that Eliot is conscious of the semantic riches to be gained by re-establishing a word in some of its lost connotations.[19] His own diction exemplifies a characteristic sensitivity toward the history of words: "No word is too new if it is the only word for the purpose; no word is too archaic if it is the only word for the purpose."[20] In his handling of vocabulary Eliot conforms to his own dictum of verbal economy in stylistics; this point of style, moreover, is well suited to the lyric form he has chosen.

In Eliot's handling of syntax one would hardly expect to find that "headstrong rush of undisciplined sentences" which he abhors. Each stanza is a syntactically integrated unit. All but the penultimate stanza comprise one complete sentence. Though this stanza has two separate sentences, the thought structure matches that of the first and last stanzas, where a strong caesura marked by a semicolon and a colon respectively sets up a relationship between the first two lines and the last three. There is actually no change in thought, but a development of the thought already presented. No stanza breaks the self-contained metrical unit to pour over into the next. This syntactic-stanzaic integrity is well suited to the lyric form, which structurally evolves from the regularity of a musical discipline.[21] Every sentence in the poem, except the one just referred to, begins in the regular subject-verb ordering, proceeding, however, with much complexity and variety. The involutions of each sentence on its way to the heavily weighted last line of the stanza weave a complex thought pattern culminating in a paradoxical statement. Thus each sentence manifests complication after setting up an expectation of simplicity by its initially straightforward syntactical arrangement. This procedure is faithful to the process of thought emerging through a lyric which restores, through contemplation, the element of mystery in a revelation worn thin by custom and familiarity. Eliot has said that "a style should follow the involutions of a mode of perceiving, registering, and digesting impressions which is also involved."[22] The poet's syntactical arrangement of sentences in this lyric is suited to the order of thought in the logical structure.

Eliot has stated, somewhat vaguely, that "there is a logic of the imagination was well as a logic of concepts."[23] One certainly sees no evidence of a dichotomy between the imagery of this poem and the thought structure. Indeed he has criticized Shelley for just such a dichotomy, for keeping his images on one side and his thoughts on another.[24] Nor does Eliot divorce imagery from emotional content, a fault he noted in Swinburne. For Eliot neither the material world nor the world of human feelings exists in Swinburne. His is a world of language; the words are peculiarly unrelated to human experience, but are sought for their own sake: "It is, in fact, the word that gives him the thrill, not the object. When you take to pieces any verse of Swinburne, you find always that the object was not there–only the word" and "the vague associations of idea that the words give him."[25] In the "East Coker" lyric, however, the images are themselves both conceptual and weighted with emotional overtones. Eliot does not merit the objection that his "feeling for language [has] outstripped his feeling for things."[26] Even if the imagery did not connote a pervading illness on a spiritual plane, it would be convincing in itself of illness on a physical level. He has described so concretely the painful process of purgation of sickness by surgery that one can perceive through this medium the reality of the spiritual condition of purgation.[27] The spiritual malady described gains intensity from the physical descriptions of an analogous bodily state. The imagery is precise. Eliot has said very early (1917) that "the vague is a more dangerous path for poetry than the arid."[28] He has not taken the dangerous course. There is nothing vague here. The very familiarity of the images precludes any possibility of their being nebulous. Eliot's imagery has the directness and simplicity he admired in Southwell,[29] yet there is an inventiveness in his use of quite traditional metaphors. It is almost a sleight-of-hand technique that could turn the familiar "divine physician" cliché into "wounded surgeon," thereby restoring the concept of freshness and vigor. The precision is unmistakable. Eliot neatly delineates the double role of Christ as Redeemer. He shares in man's suffering by his wounds; he heals man's illness by his surgery. There is, moreover, deft precision in the epithet "wounded," which neatly differentiates the cause of suffering in the surgeon from that in the patient. The surgeon's ailment is a wound inflicted from without, not a sickness within as in the case of humankind dying from fatal fever and tended by the Church. The cause of the latter's dying is not specified, probably because the Church is identified with both Christ and mankind. To specify either wounding or illness as the exclusive cause of her dying would be to limit the Church to one identification, which would not be precise.

Another piece of ingenuity is the designation of Adam as "the ruined millionaire."[30] The urbanity implied in the use of the term only enhances the freshness of such an image which yet fits perfectly into the hospital metaphor of the whole lyric. What is frequently taken for granted from overfamiliarity is thrust upon one's awareness; namely, the riches once in man's possession. The agony of loss amplifies that of simple deprivation. But there is still another aspect to the image. It underscores man's loss not only by amplification but also by irony. It is the ruin that the earth-hospital is endowed with, not the riches. It is not the millionaire, the prelapsarian Adam, but the ruined millionaire, the fallen Adam, who endows it with what is his to bequeath. This enigmatic twist heightens the whole and rejuvenates a familiar expression in an unfamiliar usage, replacing the overworn religious term of "fallen man." These are certainly examples of that "greatest economy of words and greatest austerity of metaphor, simile, verbal beauty, and elegance" which Eliot claims can be the material of great poetry.[31]

The same verbal ingenuity is used in the images describing the sickness in stanza 4. It is unusual to speak of a fever in terms of pain singing along mental wires. The placement of this image, moreover, in juxtaposition to the one describing the physical ascent of the fever from feet to knees gives the all-pervasive scope of the illness. In its economy it is similar to the splicing techniques in film-making. Yet for all the verbal economy, no descriptive detail seems to be left out. The mental aspect of the sickness is given physical expression and consequently a concreteness it would not otherwise have. The extremes of temperature epitomized in the oxymoron "frigid . . . fires" give evidence of the lack of order in this fallen state. Yet the promised order to come through this purgation is indicated by the mean in "warmed."

One further image may be singled out as a particularly original usage of a very familiar expression. It is certainly not common to speak of the Eucharist as "dripping blood" and "bloody flesh," yet it would be difficult to think of other terminology which would so graphically convey the idea of a sacrificial meal—the partaking of a sacrificed victim. The effect is the more striking when one considers that the poet here does not even use another image; he simply uses "flesh" and "blood" with two adjectives which, though integral to the things described, have connotations not associated with food and drink. In stressing flesh and blood, so modified, as food and drink he brings to consciousness a fact dulled by usage. By transforming common religious terminology, however slightly, Eliot is able to revivify the meaning behind it. In each case the heightening of the consciousness is done precisely through feeling. He makes theological concepts sensuously apprehensible.

Besides the freshness evident in the imagery, Eliot has structured the image sequence in such a way that the enigma projected in the straightforward closing of stanza 1 is amplified in each successive stanza ending. The images are, as it were, plotted so that the whole pattern forms a climactic progression culminating in the most striking enigma terminating the poem. It is by pushing the question full circle that the wounded surgeon resolves the enigma of the fever chart. Heavy use of irony intensifies the paradox described. All Eliot's language here is, of course, figurative, but the literal description is not to be ignored. In posing a humanly untenable situation he draws attention to the paradoxical temper of redemption through suffering. The spiritual death preceding rebirth is thus not underemphasized, nor is the consequent rebirth underestimated. The price is no index to the prize. So Eliot's extraordinarily illogical hospital imagery is not mere shock technique. It is an "emotional equivalent of thought." Thus one can see the force in his ironic description. The patient is under the care of a dying nurse whose sole function is to supervise his decline. The hospital is not to bring about recovery. To do well there means to die. The paternal care does not prevent death, but sees that it comes about as the ultimate goal to which the patient moves if he responds to the treatment. The enigma of the fever chart is demonstrated as such in the freezing-burning process of the disease's progress delineated in stanza 4. During all this time of purgation the patient has for food and drink the blood and flesh of a vicariously sacrificed victim. In spite of all this the puzzling involutions of the last stanza lead one to believe that the patient has not yet arrived at the state of necessary awareness. The problem is, however, unequivocally resolved in the last line. The patient would not call the day of expiation "good" if he were not aware of his need for deliverance.

The word ending the poem is supremely provocative, the climax of a series of plotted, incremental paradoxes. Placed terminally, accentually, in an unusual grammatical construction, in the rimed position, and in an inversion of a familiar and heavily overtoned phrase, "good" calls attention to itself. It would seem that Eliot has used every stylistic, grammatical, syntactical, and auditory force to intensify the significance of this word. In all the examples pointed out as ingenious manipulation of material, one of the most notable skills of the poet is his ability to exploit one expression to get several effects. The poem in its enigmatic resolution has fulfilled in meaning structure the expectations set up in the first stanza ending.

Eliot has said unequivocally that style is not the whole of poetry.[32] This is especially so if one limits the concept of style to the three points selected by Eliot as its constituents; namely, vocabulary, syntax, and order of thought There are other formal elements which must be investigated. Two properties of sound structure, metrics and rime, are particularly important to the lyric in its formal analogy to music.

"East Coker" 4 starts regularly with a heavily incantatory four-stress line. This pattern is maintained consistently for the first three lines of each stanza, expanding to five stresses for the penultimate and six for the last line. The four-stress line forms a heavy base from which the last lines of each stanza expand as the syllabic count expands.Thus, for all the hammer-beat effect, the basic stress pattern has elasticity. Nor are the expanded lines an arbitrary device. Expansion underscores the sense, because in departing from the regularity of rhythm it draws attention to the meaning of the last line, which in every stanza after the initial one is a kind of punch line involving a contradiction. Structurally, by sheer weight, this line becomes a pedestal supporting the sense of the preceding lines.

Though the stress pattern is not perfectly regular, the syllabic count exhibits perfect consistency with the model established in the first stanza. This is rare in Eliot, though he admires its use in other poets.[33] Each stanza exhibits a syllabic pattern of 8, 8, 8, 10, 12, the only possible deviation being the second line of the third stanza: "Endowed by the ruined millionaire." Whether or not it is a nine-syllable line depends on how one pronounces "ruined." Eliot's own reading indicates the word as one syllable. The syllabic pattern parallels the stress pattern in its overall effect: that of maintaining a weight emphasis at the last two lines of the stanza, which coincides with the increased weight in meaning.

One can see a correspondence in this lyric between Eliot's metrical pattern and his rime structure. The poet uses rime in the pattern *ababb,* employing a different set of chimes for each stanza while following the same scheme of alternation. Again there must be one reservation pointed out: in stanza 4 the first rime ("knees"-"freeze") is not a new sound, but repeats its corresponding sound ("disease"-"please") in stanza 2. Perfect rime dominates, but there are two departures: the quasirime "hospital"-"shall" of stanza 3, and the slant second rime of the last stanza, "food"-"blood"-"good." With the exception of the quasirime of stanza 3 mentioned above, all rimes are masculine. The accent is given an augmentation by the heavy rimes, which for the most part punctuate end-stopped lines. The dominant rime for each stanza, the one which terminates three of the five lines, encompasses the heavily weighted end lines. Rime, alternate through the stanza, doubles on the last line. The pedestal effect of metrical pattern in both stress design and syllabic count is thus echoed in the rime scheme.

If one allows for the language difference most evident in the feminine rimes of the Latin, the incantatory effect of Eliot's poem is similar to the Passion lyric "Stabat Mater." The hymnal quality in that composition lies in the sound structure whose primitive, heavily incantatory rhythm fits the elemental feelings underlying the intellectually wrought apparatus of imagery. Eliot has said that the hymn, like the epigram, is an extremely objective type of verse. It "should be charged with intense feeling, but it must be a feeling which can be completely shared."[34] This, he says, is possible only to an impersonal writer, the kind of writer Eliot praises consistently throughout his career. In "Tradition and the Individual Talent" (1919) he writes: ". . . the more perfect the artist, the more completely separate in him will be the man who suffers and the mind which creates; the more perfectly will the mind digest and transmute the passions which are its material" (*SE*, p. 7-8). In 1940 he praises Yeats as the kind of mature poet who, "out of intense and personal experience, is able to express a general truth; retaining all the particularity of his experience, to make of it a general symbol" (*PP*, p. 299). Whatever personal emotion Eliot may have experienced by his meditation on the Passion of Christ and the meaning of the Eucharist, he has transmuted into a lyric of strong precision and objectivity.

One sees here a balance of intellect and sensibility within an ambient of stylistic and auditory correspondence—"The complete consort dancing together." The principle of organization is what Eliot prizes in Ben Jonson precisely because it is this principle to which he attributes the control of emotion and its integration into the intellectual appeal. In Jonson "no swarms of inarticulate feelings are aroused. The immediate appeal of Jonson is to the mind; his emotional tone is not in the single verse, but in the design of the whole."[35] It is in the design of the whole and the integration of its parts that Eliot has achieved the intellect-sensibility fusion which makes the matter of this religious lyric communicable as feeling completely shared and as thought sensuously apprehended.

"LITTLE GIDDING" 4

The dove descending breaks the air
With flame of incandescent terror
Of which the tongues declare
The one discharge from sin and error.
The only hope, or else despair
    Lies in the choice of pyre or pyre–
    To be redeemed from fire by fire.

Who then devised the torment? Love.
Love is the unfamiliar Name
Behind the hands that wove
The intolerable shirt of flame
Which human power cannot remove.
    We only live, only suspire
    Consumed by either fire or fire.

In the terza rima section of "Little Gidding" 2 the last words of the dead master to the poet concern purgation:

From wrong to wrong the exasperated spirit
    Proceeds, unless restored by that refining fire
    Where you must move in measure like a dancer.

Eliot certainly moves through "East Coker" 4 in measure. The same regularity marks his other purgation lyric in the fourth section of "Little Gidding." According to Eliot's canon it is fitting that form and content should fuse, and since he identifies the subject of purgation with measured motion, it is natural that his verses on that subject should be highly structured. Consequently the same formal discipline that marked the "East Coker" lyric is in evidence in "Little Gidding" 4.

Metrically there is the same heavily incantatory effect of the almost consistently sustained four-stress line, while the seven-line stanza moves with determination through alternating rime down to the equipoised final couplet. Though the couplet maintains the same prosodic weight consistency as the preceding lines, it is set off by indentation as a special structural unit, and the rime scheme reinforces the separation by introducing the unused *c* rime to the last two lines. The rime, moreover, by linking the two couplets in sound, emphasizes their close relationship in meaning. This special structural feature of the couplet is analogous to the expanded weight feature of the corresponding end lines in the "East Coker" stanzas. In both cases the structure intensifies the meaning, and each structure differs insofar as the meaning conveyed is different. In "East Coker" the weighted end-lines function to resolve all the enigmas in the meaning structure. The couplets in "Little Gidding," however, hold in tension each ambivalence of meaning. Balance, not resolution, is the technique, and every element of this short lyric mirrors this function so obvious in the couplet.

The stylistic features of the poem likewise resemble those of "East Coker" 4. The poet follows the same type of verbal economy in diction, the same syntactical integration of stanzaic units, the same carefully constructed order of thought. There is, however, a difference commensurate with the variant aspect under which he sees purgation in this lyric. The main idea of both poems is that suffering must be undergone if deliverance is to be reached, and this fact is given to man in the form of a revelation. But the "Little Gidding" lyric is once removed both as to the manner of revelation and the manner of suffering prescribed. It is no longer the traditionally divine institution speaking for the divinity; it is an institution anything but divine: war comes out of the inherent human sickness described in "East Coker" 4. The suffering is not just endurance of one's own illness, but of pain inflicted from without, from the collective illness of mankind disordered. It is the growing worse referred to in the earlier lyric. In "East Coker" 4 one did well by simple resignation; in "Little Gidding" 4 active choice is demanded. It is precisely this disparity that warrants the difference in the formal pattern. Progression of thought in "East Coker" 4 was marked by a series of climactic enigmas reaching a zenith at the terminal line. A five-stanza structure could provide the necessary scope for such progressive movement of thought. It would not be suitable for the thought pattern of "Little Gidding" 4, which emphasizes choice between alternatives and consequently needs an equipoised formal structure. Comprising two stanzaic divisions, the whole lyric is built on a system of duals, most obviously focused in the couplet ending each stanza. There the choice is given explicit verbal expression in exactly matching pairs of terms: "pyre"-"pyre," "fire"-"fire." The exact repetition to designate choice of alternatives underscores their surface similarity—suffering is suffering no matter what the cause. At the same time the technique ironically intensifies the disparity between them, given explicitly in the set of opposites that precede the first couplet and designate the antithesis: "hope"-"despair."

There are two principal images in the poem, each contained in its separate stanza and each having a dual perspective. Both are images of pain, and both are regulated by outside forces. Love is involved in both, and in both love is depicted in an ambivalent role. Each uses a traditional image in a way quite at variance with tradition, yet embodying all the associations of that tradition for its own ends. The dove, traditionally associated with the Holy Spirit, the spirit of love who descended in tongues of fire, is here an enemy aircraft whose tongues of fire, nevertheless, proclaim a form of deliverance from sin and error. The diction integral to the image here very closely enhances the duality and ambivalence, showing that Eliot is quite conscious of the possibilities of his language and very much aware of the meaning of every word he uses.[36] The noun "discharge" can be taken in two ways. As an emission of gunfire, it fits the fighter plane image perfectly. No less perfectly does it fit the traditional dove image in its other sense of acquittal, of freeing one from a charge held against him. The verb "declare" likewise has a double sense, each aspect of which fits the meaning here. The sense of "declare" as making a formal announcement clearly and plainly has a pertinence which is certainly underscored by the tongue image. But "declare" also has the sense of a showing forth, a manifestation through facts and circumstance. Both senses inhere in Eliot's use of the image, and both are held in balance. What the tongues are declaring is precisely the incendiary terror they are releasing. Either way is fire: one of destruction and despair, the other of purgation and hope. Choice of the latter redeems the chooser from the former. In choosing the word "pyre" to designate alternatives, Eliot has made by association a suitable link with the next stanza. Hercules was delivered from the tormenting fire of the Nessus shirt by mounting his own funeral pyre.

The same counterpoise technique evident in the first stanza governs the image of the second, whose immediate relation to the first is set up by the interrogative form of its opening. If there has been any doubt about the dove image having the traditional overtones of love, it is dispelled here. Love, which significantly chimes with the beginning of the first line of the first stanza, is explicitly mentioned, and comprising as it does a single long syllable after a heavy caesura, there can be no doubt about the poet's intention of emphasizing what he calls "the unfamiliar Name." Love is specifically identified as the deviser of the torment. Moreover the torment itself is described here in terms of the Nessus shirt, a particularly difficult image to assimilate into an ambient of divine love because of its associations. Indeed all the traditional associations of its devising have to be turned inside out in the process of its assimilation to the poem. The shirt of myth was devised by hatred, not love; and it was given to its wearer out of misguided love. By association, then, the poet produces here an effect analogous to that of the war image in the first stanza. Both stanzas culminate in a statement of choice between two alternative forms of suffering: fire or fire—the fire of sin and despair or the fire of love redeeming through purgation into hope. By designating in stanza 1 the immediate cause of wartime devastation as "dove," the poet implies the ultimate cause as divine love. He does the same in stanza 2 by naming Love explicitly as the inventor of the shirt of flame, a phenomenon one associates with hatred and revenge. In both cases the love reference lies behind the immediate references. In both cases, therefore, the dubiety of the image is suitable. A double focus is needed, for in both cases the suffering is attributed to divine love as its cause, whereas its immediate cause is not love at all, but sin. It is this sin, not purgation, from which man is redeemed.

> Sin is Behovely, but
> All shall be well, and
> All manner of thing shall be well.

If the images of suffering did not so clearly designate sin, and if they did fit more reasonably into the ambient of divine love to which they are attributed, one might confuse the suffering here described with that of purgation itself. The necessity of choice as the lodestone transforming suffering into purgation would be lost, and the structure of the poem would be nonorganic. Within the whole pattern of *Four Quartets* the lyric would be no more than a simple repetition of "East Coker" 4 instead of a very important incremental repetition of the purgation theme.

In an apparent confusion and blurring of focus, then, the poet actually exhibits great precision. In using traditional material for his own ends, he is able to abstract what is directly to his purpose and use what is not directly assimilable as a catalyst. The effect produced by such counterpointing is startling. It is that "pleasure in sudden transference" Eliot so much admires in Andrew Marvell. "Two things very different are brought together, and the spark of ecstasy generated in us is a perception of power in bringing them together."[37] The unassimilable material holds its own; it is not just absorbed harmoniously into the whole. But it is just this independent play against the love-ordered cosmos that is needed. A dichotomy must be recognized and held. There are two fires ordered to two different ends. The tension of choice is maintained in both structure and diction.

Eliot has set up in this lyric an extraordinary rhythm of structural parts and stylistic elements. This is the kind of rhythm he described in one of his early articles: "Rhythm, of course, is a highly personal matter; it is not a verse-form. It is always the real pattern in the carpet, the scheme of organization of thought, feeling, and vocabulary, the way in which everything comes together."[38] The scheme of organization in the poem is functional because the poet has used all the materials selected in such a way that they all inform not only the subject chosen but also the particular aspect under which he chooses to consider it. Bearing a striking resemblance to "East Coker" 4, the "Little Gidding" lyric varies just as strikingly in several points. In each case the similarity seems attributable to the fact that both poems are on the same purgatorial subject, while the difference seems to spring directly from the disparate focus of each poem on that subject. The same principle operates in both: a fusion of technique and meaning. One feels that Eliot has "found an idiom and a metric perfectly suited for what [he] had to say."[39]

"BURNT NORTON" 4

Time and the bell have buried the day,
The black cloud carries the sun away.
Will the sunflower turn to us, will the clematis
Stray down, bend to us; tendril and spray
Clutch and cling?
Chill
Fingers of yew be curled
Down on us? After the kingfisher's wing
Has answered light to light, and is silent, the light is still
At the still point of the turning world.

Because Eliot is so conscious of assimilation of the parts into the whole, he frequently considers the possibilities of musical analogy in the description of poetic composition. Though he is aware of certain dangers in pushing musical analogy too far, he sees its value.[40] To him, the word "music" is an apt literary term because of its connotations of structure and rhythm, the relation of the parts to the whole that inhere in musical composition. His concept of music in poetry involves much more than just the sounds of words. When he uses the word "musical" to describe any linguistic element, he refers to a certain relationship which that element has to the total structure. Under such a method of consideration there is no element of a poem which cannot be described in terms of some musical analogy. Consequently he can speak of the "music of imagery" as well as sound, and can say that the pattern of imagery forms a "very complex musical structure."[41] This principle of the musical structure of imagery can be seen operating in the "East Coker" and "Little Gidding" lyrics in conjunction with all the other elements of the poems. In "Burnt Norton" 4, however, Eliot plies a different technique by which the structure of imagery and the structure of sound do not coincide. Metric, rime, and syntax function independently of one another, and none of these elements operates in complete alignment with the imagery. This poem displays less semantic density than either of the other two lyrics, but shows more complication in sound structure where all the elements play against one another to produce a curious music. An apparently irregular metrical construct turns out upon examination to be loosely patterned. The ten-line, one-stanza poem is bifurcated by a curious metrical system in which the number of stresses in the lines decreases as they move toward the center and increases again as they approach the end of the poem. This weight distribution is certainly not one of any regularity (4 5 5 5 2 1 4 4 6 4), though the four-stress line does dominate. The cadence pattern is one of dominantly falling rhythm, but of much irregularity in the type of foot. The number of feet to a line (4 4 5 4 2 1 2 4 6 4) does not correspond exactly to the number of stresses; thus, line 4 comprises only four feet because of the initial spondee, and line 7 presents a particularly difficult problem in Eliot's oral reading. The scansion of the line would seem to be:

/ x x / x /
"Fingers of yew be curled," comprising one falling and two rising feet. Eliot, however, reads it as / x x / / /, with the verse falling distinctly into two units, one a dactyl, the other a three-stress single foot. Another factor which contributes to the overall effect of irregularity is Eliot's use of the run-on line. After the first two verses all the lines except 5 and 10 are enjambed. There seems to be no system in his cadence pattern except the dominance of falling meter throughout.

The rime follows a more regular scheme in which the first four lines form one unit, *aaba,* while the last six lines use a different set of rimes in the pattern *cdecde.* The division of this bipartite rime system, however, does not coincide with the prosodic center in the monosyllabic sixth line, and no relationship between the two systems is discernible. The total effect of rime placement is curious. Because of the great disparity in line length the rimes do not recur with spatial regularity. The expectation of regularity set up in the first two lines where rime, rhythm, and syntax all coordinate is not maintained. It seems as though Eliot is employing a rime which forms a pattern *against* the metric and sense patterns which he notes in other contemporary poets and to which he does not object.[42]

Syntactically the poem comprises three sentences, an interrogative enveloped by two declarative statements.[43] But just as there is no relationship between the bipartite prosodic weight division at line 6 and the two parts of the rime system separating at lines 4 and 5, neither is there any apparent connection between either of these systems and the syntactic units. There is not a harmonious coinciding of self-contained units, but rather an interplay of each against the other like "metrical schemes in a kind of counterpoint."[44] Eliot relies on his structure of imagery for a control, if not a fusion, of this curious system of disparately patterned sound and stylistic elements. The imagery is so integral to the thought and to the whole organization of the poem that one begins to understand what Eliot means when he speaks of the "music of imagery" as forming a disciplined structure of its own and acting as a unifying force among the various elements.

In this musical use of imagery Eliot very much resembles George Herbert. Many times in his prose essays Eliot has expressed admiration for Herbert as lyric poet. He notes particularly his "resourcefulness of invention" which produced so many "exquisite variations of form" in *The Temple.* He attributes in some measure this mastery of lyric verse to Herbert's knowledge of and training in music, both choral and instrumental.[45] Though Eliot disclaims for himself any such technical training in music,[46] yet it is noteworthy that he can produce within *Four Quartets* a lyric variety of his own, though certainly on a much smaller scale than Herbert. His variety of formal pattern, moreover, indicates variations of meaning as it does in Herbert.[47]

Eliot's poem if printed in the manner of many of Herbert's would form on the page the shape of an hourglass, and it may not be too farfetched to see a stylistic analogy between the "Burnt Norton" lyric and Herbert's "Easter Wings," which cuts the same hourglass shape both in print and in style. Herbert's poem, even if it were not printed so as to form two sets of wings curiously sideways on the page, would structurally simulate that very shape. It is the shape, so to speak, of the meaning itself and of all the constituents of that meaning. The motion of Herbert's stanza is down and up, the falling and rising of something in flight. The first stanza begins with man's creation in wealth, and in recounting his loss of that wealth the lines decrease successively by one cadence each until a single spondaic foot is reached at the central point where man is described as "Most poore." The next line, also consisting of one significantly rising foot, "With thee," begins an upward thrust in sense as well as sound. The succeeding lines move out by one foot each as the image of the lark's flight is absorbed into the flight of man's spiritual victory in Christ's rising. The metrical statistics of Herbert's poem are vital; they mirror the rhythm of the imagery which carries the thought order of man's fall and Christ's lifting up of him.

In Eliot's lyric something similar occurs, though of necessity differing from the total integration of all elements into a perfectly harmonious structure. In Herbert's poem the downward-upward motion of the sense carried by the images is perfectly mirrored in the prosodic structure. The sense of "Burnt Norton" 4, however, moves only downward, and the images carrying that thought structure move in that direction throughout. The prosodic structure, on the other hand, moves toward a diminution at the center of the poem and an augmentation as the lines reach the end, resembling, though irregularly, the general hourglass movement of Herbert's poem. It would seem at first that there is no connection in "Burnt Norton" 4 between the prosodic structure and the sense structure carried on in the images. On closer inspection, however, one sees a rendition in meter of a motion implied by the images. At the beginning of the lyric the images are high: the bell which marks time, the black cloud, and the sun are all images of the air. The fact that the day is "buried" prepares for the earth images which follow: sunflower, clematis, yew. Not only does the focus move from air to earth, but there is also a downward bending of all earth images. The sunflower's turning to us from its usual orientation is a movement downward. The clematis also is to "stray down" in bending to us. Even the yew is designated as curling down to reach us. The word "buried" in line 1 starts the downward motion in a lyric whose whole sense is governed by "down," significantly repeated once. Even the image of the kingfisher, whose "wing / has answered light to light and is silent," is introduced in terms of cessation of flight, a settling down for the night. All things converge to the still point, the source of light where the light is stored. Thus the direct motion of the images of "Burnt Norton" 4 is invariably down. Yet the images used imply an ensuing motion upward. *Up* is the undersense of such images as trees, climbing vines, sunflowers.

The whole lyric is concerned with the coming on of night. The light is dying at the end of the day. Day is being buried. The sunflower drooping at sunset implies a resurgence at dawn's restoration of the light. The downward motion of a climbing vine suggests the blossom and seed time, the time of fullness which promises a new life of climbing growth. The last plant image, yew, has double connotation as symbol of death but also of immortality. The former is certainly conveyed in the immediate description of the yew with its chill fingers curled down on us. But as soon as the question of mortality is asked, the kingfisher's wing, though stilled at sundown, nevertheless implies a lifting of the poem into another realm beyond mortality. The kingfisher–bird of the winter solstice, halcyon bird of the calm–is a traditional symbol of Christ. There is here, then, as in "Easter Wings," a resurrection from the dead implied. All the images move toward the still point, the point where the light is stored, inherent promise of a new day. If this is not expressed, the implication is visible in Eliot's choice of objects. It is paradoxically in this implied motion and implied meaning that one sees an integration of the prosodic pattern with the structure of meaning. The design in the line length carries out explicitly the further sense implied by the completely downward motion of images to the still center where any ensuing motion must be up.

In his essay "The Music of Poetry" Eliot has remarked: "It may be possible that the beauty of some English poetry is due to the presence of more than one metrical structure in it." In the same essay he notes that "there are possibilities for verse which bear some analogy to the development of a theme by different groups of instruments" (*PP*, pp. 20, 32). In "Burnt Norton" 4 this seems to be the technique. The various sound-structures, while not apparently blending with one another, do each help to develop the theme by playing against and thus enhancing the imagery which carries the thought pattern in its downward motion to the still point, implying a subsequent resurrection. The interplay of structures is intricate. The dominantly falling cadence parallels the downward motion of the imagery. This falling rhythm is maintained with deliberation and much technical acumen, even in the interrogative midsection. Here the natural rise expected in an interrogative structure plays against the downward trend of the cadences which are producing a motion in sympathy with the earthward bent of the images. The prosodic structure at first mirrors this downward sense, but goes on to simulate the upward motion implicit in the images themselves. Rime is the only element which does not seem to have any functional need for its two-part division coming where it does. Its counterpoint plays against each of the other structures, never really resolving into any one of them, not even the imagery. In an ambient of counterpoint it seems fitting that at least one of the elements producing it should be left free to carry the effect through to the end. Rime, disparately placed temporally because of the variant line lengths, and somewhat obscured in the almost continual enjambment after the first two verses, asserts itself by not lending its pattern to a systematic structural fusion. In this way the poet has kept the images and the music as two things and not one thing with simply a suggestion of each. Eliot considered this an important feature of song for which he praises Campion.[48]

Eliot's handling of structure follows a complicated pattern in which each system can be heard distinct from the others and yet contributes in a unique way to the thought pattern inherent in the imagery. It is indeed a musical structure by Eliot's standards, for there is an orientation of parts to whole. In this lyric the method is polyphonic rather than harmonic. But there is a dominant strain which the other elements either more or less resolve themselves into or else play themselves against: the structure of imagery which carries the structure of meaning.

"THE DRY SALVAGES" 4

Lady, whose shrine stands on the promontory,
Pray for all those who are in ships, those
Whose business has to do with fish, and
Those concerned with every lawful traffic
And those who conduct them.

Repeat a prayer also on behalf of
Women who have seen their sons or husbands
Setting forth, and not returning:
Figlia del tuo figlio,
Queen of Heaven.

> Also pray for those who were in ships, and
> Ended their voyage on the sand, in the sea's lips
> Or in the dark throat which will not reject them
> Or wherever cannot reach them the sound of the sea bell's
> Perpetual angelus.

The prayer to the Virgin in the fourth section of "The Dry Salvages" is the only lyric in the form of direct address. It does not, however, have the hymnlike quality that measures the rhythms of the "East Coker" and "Little Gidding" lyrics. It does not even have the songlike quality of "Burnt Norton" 4, which so resembles, in its opening two lines at least, the refrain of a medieval secular lyric, "The baily beareth the bell away." The prayer to the Virgin in "The Dry Salvages" is the only lyric of the four that approaches the so-called free verse style, a subject on which Eliot has had much to say in the course of the years. Most of his theory is formulated quite early and quite emphatically in an article appearing in the *New Statesman* in 1917.[49] He considers vers libre a "preposterous fiction." As far as Eliot is concerned, it does not exist. "If *vers libre* is a genuine verse-form it will have a positive definition. And I can define it only in negatives: (1) absence of pattern, (2) absence of rhyme, (3) absence of meter" (p. 518). However unfair such a definition is to the defenders of vers libre, it is Eliot's critical view and may be used as an index of his own practice at least.

If "The Dry Salvages" 4 is measured against this negative definition, it will not qualify as free verse. For one thing there is a definite pattern of formal structure. The poem is divided into three stanzas of five lines, each forming one syntactic unit, a completed sentence. The formal address opening each stanza is marked by a syntactical repetition slightly varied: "Pray for," "Repeat a prayer," "Also pray for." The first formal address ushers in a prayer for merchant sailors. There is no emotion discernible in the pedestrian language in which it is encased. The solemnity, however, is unmistakable in the anaphoric structure: "those who are in ships," "those / Whose business," "Those concerned," "those who conduct." In the second strophe the formal prayer is for the bereaved women, certainly a subject with emotional overtones. Yet it is a notably unemotional diction that is employed here. Not one adjective except the possessive "their" is used. The stanza relies on associative technique for its emotional effect, reflecting as it does the first section of "The Dry Salvages," where the plight of the "anxious worried women / Lying awake" is given an explicit delineation, and where the bell closing part 1 ushers in the remotely sestina-like dirge of the "last annunciation." The high point of the stanza is of course the quotation from *Paradiso* 33.1, where the Virgin Mother is addressed in terms which encompass a double relationship on behalf of women who are doubly bereaved. The simple prayer is thus given a solemnity associated with St. Bernard's address to Mary in the last canto of the *Comedy.* By association too the richness of the address is intensified, for in Bernard's prayer the Virgin Mother is called "the noonday torch of charity" among the blessed and "the living spring of Hope" among mortals below.[50] In her womb was rekindled the love by whose warmth the multifoliate rose blossoms in eternal peace and eternal union.[51] In this love there is no separation. By the Dantesque association, then, the prayer of section 4 resolves into hope and peace "the hardly, barely prayable / Prayer of the one Annunciation" which closed the sestina section of part 2. This resolution is likewise projected into the closing of the next stanza, which refers specifically to the Annunciation prayer, the angelus.

The third formal address to Mary opening stanza 3 is for the shipwrecked. By grammatical parallelism–"those who were in ships" echoing "those who are in ships" of stanza 1–it is immediately tied in with the anaphoric structure of the first stanza. The third strophe, moreover, has syntactic parallelism of its own: first, in the repeated designation of place by a prepositional phrase "in ships," "on the sand," "in the sea's lips," "in the dark throat"; second, in the anaphoric use of "Or" at the beginning of the third and fourth lines. Grammatical repetition works as a unifying factor in a poem of apparently free and even prosaic structure. It governs the rhythm and functions in the meaning structure as a climactic parallelism signalling a development of emotional content as the poem shifts from the distantly impersonal focus of stanza 1 to the agony of the bereaved in stanza 2, to the personally tragic outcome of the sea voyagers in stanza 3.

By the second negative criterion for free verse, the prayer of section 4 might at first glance appear to qualify. The lyric is obviously a nonriming poem. Eliot notes in his criticism the contemporary tendency either to dispense with rime altogether, or "to make a pattern directly in contrast with the sense and rhythm pattern, to give a greater intricacy."[52] In "Burnt Norton" 4 he took the latter course; in "The Dry Salvages" the former seems to be the method. It is not surprising that Eliot would eliminate rime even from a lyric verse. As early as the 1917 essay on vers libre, he observed: "It is possible that excessive devotion to rhyme has thickened the modern ear. . . . The rejection of rhyme is not a leap at facility; on the contrary, it imposes a much severer strain upon the language. When the comforting echo of rhyme is removed, success or failure in the choice of words, in the sentence structure, in the order, is at once held up to the standards of prose" (*New Statesman,* p. 519). Of the four lyric sections, "The Dry Salvages" 4 is certainly the one nearest to prose. This is noteworthy, considering the rich tradition of lyrics to the Virgin in Western literature.[53]

Eliot's line endings, devoid of rimes as they are, employ a substitute technique of chiming cadence in the consistency of their feminine endings.[54] The fact that feminine endings are not usual in English only calls attention to the falling cadence. To maintain this consistency the poet has had recourse, in a way, to something he had complained about in certain minor Elizabethans. He severely criticized Cyril Tourneur's tendency "to polish off a fair line of iambics even at the cost of amputating a preposition from its substantive" (p. 519). Since Eliot, moreover, is not trying to polish off a fair line of iambics, his own practice seems less excusable than that of the blank verse writer who had to cope with the exigencies of a more rigid metrical pattern. Eliot's syntactical splitting at line endings may seem arbitrary until one sees the total unifying effect of the feminine endings which could hardly be attained in any way more straightforward and simple than they are here. There are, moreover, only six lines (2, 3, 6, 7, 11, 14) in which grammatical units are separated by enjambment. In only one of these (6) does the poet separate a preposition from its object. Two lines (3, 11) end with "and," thereby separating the conjunction from one of its coordinates. One line ending (2) separates a relative pronoun "whose" from its antecedent "those." In one case (7) the substantives are separated from their verbal modifiers; in another (11) the noun is cut off from its possessive modifier. Six such lines are not excessive in a fifteen-line poem.

Though the lyric is devoid of rime, it nevertheless attains its repetitive effects by other means. The structural device of anaphora noted above has a solemn incantatory effect of its own which substitutes in one way for the missing rime. The consistently maintained feminine endings give a lyric delicacy of cadence chime to an otherwise prosaic form of address. Rime, missing from the poem, is compensated for by two other techniques of sound repetition, one grammatical, the other metrical.

The third Eliot hallmark of vers libre is absence of meter. An examination of "The Dry Salvages" lyric in this light reveals many interesting things. Of the four lyrics this is the most difficult to scan. But Eliot has little respect for scansion as such. "There is," he says, "no reason why, within the single line there should be any repetition; why there should not be lines (as there are) divisible only into feet of different types" (*New Statesman,* p. 518). That Eliot does not put much stock in a system of scansion, however, does not warrant the conclusion that he despises meter itself. On the contrary he specifies quite categorically: "There is no escape from meter; there is only mastery" (p. 519). He considers it a capital error for a poet "not to have conceived the simple truth that *some* artificial limitation is necessary" (p. 519). His own metrics in this lyric are not so irregular as to be without any form of artificial limitation. While there is absolutely no regularity discernible in the syllabic structure, each stanza approaches some sort of regularity in the distribution of feet. The verses are dominantly of four cadences with a dimeter line terminating each stanza. To each stanza there is one five-stress line variously placed, while the second stanza has a singularity in the three-stress penultimate line of Italian. It is at first difficult to determine whether the whole effect is one of rising or falling rhythm. One of the main problems in scansion is Eliot's severing of metrical as well as grammatical units by his enjambment in lines 2, 3, 11. This phenomenon, which performs a valuable musical function at the line endings, nevertheless presents difficulty in scansion, because the end cadence thus produced overlaps the meaning cadence. One cannot therefore determine the foot types simply on the basis of the verse unit. But if one counts in terms of textual pause indicated by punctuation, a working principle can be established for determining the presence of anacruses and catalexes, factors of prime importance both for the division of feet and the establishing of their quality as rising or falling. By this method the lines are seen to fit into a falling pattern, dominantly trochaic, which accords well with the prominently feminine end cadences already noted. Eliot claims all verse can be scanned, but a prosodic analysis of this particular poem leads one to the conclusion that, in this case at least, "scansion tells us very little" (p. 519).

If it tells us little, that little is nevertheless important, for the scansion does point out the fact that Eliot has some form of artificial limitation behind his verse. He has been doing what he calls stretching, contracting, and distorting the traditional meter, a technique which Eliot says he learned from the later Elizabethans and from Jules Laforgue. In claiming this discipleship, Eliot was precisely refuting the charge of those who classed him as a writer of free verse.[55] In the 1917 essay he says: "The most interesting verse which has yet been written in our language has been done either by taking a very simple form, like the iambic pentameter, and constantly withdrawing from it, or taking no form at all, and constantly approximating to a very simple one" (p. 518). Farther on in the same essay he formulates this principle figuratively: "The ghost of some simple meter should lurk behind the arras in even the 'freest' verse; to advance menacingly as we doze, and withdraw when it appears against the background of an artificial limitation." What identifiable metrical ghost is lurking behind this accumulated fifteen lines of verse, it is difficult to determine. Sheer count uncovers it as certainly a falling rhythm, dominantly trochaic tetrameter, but only by a weak majority. It certainly does not have much chance "to advance menacingly" to impose itself on the whole texture of the lyric. The poet certainly has held it at bay by that "unperceived evasion of monotony" which Eliot considers "the very life of verse" (p. 518).

By Eliot's standards "The Dry Salvages" lyric is not free verse. There is a formal pattern marked by coinciding stanzaic divisions and syntactic unity, while both are underscored by anaphoric technique. While there is an absence of formal rime, it is substituted for by a consistently maintained feminine end cadence which the poet has manipulated his grammatical and metrical units to obtain. The constant suppression of regularity in metrics nowhere denotes an absence of meter, but rather a "skillful evasion" of trochaic tetrameter. Eliot's denial of the existence of free verse at all is based on his inability to see any positive definition for it, and he concludes his line of argument without altering his position: "And as for *vers libre,* we conclude that it is not defined by absence of pattern or absence of rhyme, for other verse is without these; that it is not defined by non-existence of meter, since even the *worst* verse can be scanned; and we conclude that the division between Conservative Verse and *Vers Libre* does not exist, for there is only good verse, bad verse, and chaos" (p. 519). A satisfactory definition of free verse, like a satisfactory definition of lyric verse, may never be forthcoming in literary criticism; but by Eliot's threefold negative defintion of the phenomenon, "The Dry Salvages" lyric does not qualify as vers libre.

One can see in these fourth-section poems adherence to a lyric tradition of measured verse transmuting thoughts and sentiments into concrete language. In Eliot's particular manipulation of this tradition there is continual departure from "worn-out poetical fashion." The total effect is one of genuine originality coupled with heavy reminiscences of the past. The tradition is there, but so is the freshness of something new. As Eliot remarks of Pound, so one could say of Eliot himself: "His versification is a *logical* development of the verse of his English predecessors."[56] Each of the poems is characterized by a more or less tight metrical discipline, the degree of this discipline depending on its fitness to the subject. The prosodic pattern, both in line weight and cadence type, is equally suited to the meaning structure. The poet's choice of diction and syntax seems to fuse with his order of thought, which is carried by a system of carefully worked imagery. The fourth-section lyrics are well-made poems "where every word is at home, / Taking its place to support the others." In short, the lyric variety so noticeable among the four selections can be attributed to the exigencies of handling the different subject matter of each.

One of Eliot's early principles that has not changed in his body of scattered essays is his insistence with Pope that "the sound must seem an echo to the sense." Always he doubts "whether the *sound* of two poems can be very similar, when the *sense* is entirely different."[57] He maintains that rhythm and diction produce their effect in unity, that incantation and meaning, sound and sense are inseparable.[58] Yet he continually emphasizes the duty of the poet not to depart from common speech. This must always be the norm for the poet's language. Consequently Eliot is cautious about

Valéry's assimilation of poetry to music because such assimilation overlooks its foundation in speech.[59] Milton comes under a similar censure because his "syntax is determined by the musical significance, by the auditory imagination, rather than by the attempt to follow actual speech or thought."[60] Eliot does not hesitate to use the weight of the *OED* against one poet to demonstrate that "in his choice of the word which has the right *sound,* Poe is by no means careful that it should also have the right *sense.*"[61] In 1928 Eliot had praised Ezra Pound for just this balance between sound and sense, between poetic diction and common speech. Pound, he says, learned from the poets he selected to influence him "the importance of *verse as speech* . . . and the importance of *verse as song.*"[62] He likewise praises Donne, who "first made it possible to think in lyric verse" by introducing into the lyric the natural and conversational style perfected by the Elizabethan dramatists. He notes that Donne introduced this style "in a variety of rhythms and stanza schemes which forms an inexhaustible subject of study; and at the same time retained a quality of song and the suggestion of the instrumental accompaniment of the earlier lyric."[63] It is precisely this combination of qualities that Eliot admires.

While the language of a poem must conform for better or worse to the speech patterns of contemporary usage, so must the structure of a poem be a fidelity to the thought and feeling expressed therein. "As this fidelity induces variety of thought and feeling, so it induces variety of music."[64] For all his caution concerning musical analogy, remarks on the musical qualities of verse are ubiquitous in Eliot, and they are of a piece. Most of his theory on this matter is recapitulated in his 1942 lecture "The Music of Poetry."[65] He insists that the "musical poem is a poem which has a musical pattern of sound and a musical pattern of the secondary meanings of the words which compose it, and . . . these two patterns are indissoluble and one." Sound to Eliot is just "as much an abstraction from the poem as is the sense" (p. 26). He speaks of the music of a word and says it is "at a point of intersection": its music concerns the connotative definition, its associations, its allusiveness; its music inheres in the word's relation to structure (p. 25). Certainly it is this type of music Eliot consciously employs in the diction of the *Four Quartets* lyrics, just as it is a "very complex musical structure" of imagery which he plies in each of these poems. He reminds us "that the music of verse is not a line-by-line matter, but a question of the whole poem" (p. 30). Always there is this insistence on relation of the element to the whole. It is no wonder, then, that Eliot believes the properties of music which concern the poet most nearly are "the sense of rhythm and the sense of structure" (p. 32). Both of these are concerned with the whole fabric, the relation of part to whole and whole to part.

Eliot's practice in making these lyrics is in keeping with principles constantly reiterated in his scattered critical essays. It seems quite reasonable to apply to his literary work, both poetry and prose, what he said of Ezra Pound: ". . . of no other poet can it be more important to say, that his criticism and his poetry, his precept and his practice, compose a single *oeuvre.* It is necessary to read [Eliot's] poetry to understand his criticism, and to read his criticism to understand his poetry."[66]

CHAPTER FIVE

THE FUNCTION OF LYRICS IN *FOUR QUARTETS*

The purpose of having gone into so much detailed analysis of these four short lyrics is to see *how* they mean what they do and thus to gain some idea of Eliot's technical skill and mastery in handling the lyric genre. Such an assessment is needed, moreover, if one is to ascertain the significance of each particular lyric to the meaning of its respective quartet. For it is not just that these lyrics, separately considered, are of high intrinsic merit, though it is eminently clear they are: it is precisely their integral place of function within the total body that makes them even more remarkable. Eliot used his fourth sections not simply as lyric interludes in a philosophical meditation, but rather as distillations of the entire content of each separate quartet. Moreover, a contemplation of these lyrics in succession shows that the fourth-section lyrics are very truly a "concentration without elimination" of *Four Quartets* as a whole.

For Eliot the parts of a longer poem are not separate entities, but mutually integral:

> These parts can form a whole which is more than the sum of its parts; a whole such that the pleasure we derive from the reading of any part is enhanced by our own grasp of the whole. It follows also that in the long poem some parts may be deliberately planned to be less "poetic" than the others: these passages may show no luster when extracted, but may be intended to elicit, by contrast, the significance of other parts. A long poem may gain the widest possibile variation of intensity.[1]

One sees this exemplified to great advantage in *Four Quartets.* It is plain that Eliot is using a wide variation of intensity as a vehicle to meaning. The fourth movements are, as it were, embodiments of the concepts discussed and pondered in the longer sections. Though each quartet has another notable lyric opening part 2, this lyric is not self-contained either in structure or meaning. Not only is it structurally part of a longer section, but it is also still part of the commentary or exposition of the philosophical themes constituting the large poem. Each one plays with a particular aspect of the theme and puts it into a language different in its lyricism from what goes before and after, thus giving a greater intensity to the concept under consideration. But none of these lyrics completely embodies the central points of its particular quartet. That is the function of the fourth-part lyrics, and they perform that function with brilliance.

Eliot's theological view in *Four Quartets* is one deeply felt and difficult to commit to words. The fact that three of his fifth sections are concerned with the problem of words is an indication of how much store he set by the seriousness of the difficulties involved in communication. He is attempting to communicate in language his perception of life in the dimensions of past, present, and future; the significance of history to the individual; and the leavening power of the individual on the process of history. What Eliot had seen as the significance of the individual talent to the whole body of tradition (*SE,* pp. 3–11), he now probes in regard to man in time and space, man in the history of mankind and in salvation history.

Such a perception of the meaning of life is necessary if man is to fulfill himself spiritually. Man needs to see himself in relation to everything: to the rest of creation, to his contemporaries, to mankind in history, to God. Eliot's contention in *Four Quartets* is that this perception, which constitutes the fullness of human life, is granted only intermittently in flashes of insight. The source is outside the self and can only be prepared for by a kind of vigilance, an attempt to concern oneself with a discovery of the meaning of human existence in all its relations: the idea "Of belonging to another, or to others, or to God" ("East Coker" 2). Implementation of such perspective demands self-abnegation, for to place oneself in relation to another involves a continual relinquishment of self-interest and an orientation to the other. Because of the cost of sustaining such an orientation, few strive consciously to live on the level of awareness granted momentarily in the flashes of insight received from time to time.

This moment of insight, this inbreak, appears in *The Waste Land* in the "damp gust bringing rain"; in the threefold message of the thunder; in the reiterated directive "Those are pearls that were his eyes." It totally informs "Ash Wednesday" and forms the subject matter for "Marina." Gerontion, confronted with its costliness, rejects it and faces old age with the horrifying question: "After such knowledge, what forgiveness?" Throughout his poetry Eliot is haunted by the implications for those who fail to respond to those moments of truth: "Between the idea / And the reality . . .

/ Falls the Shadow" ("The Hollow Men" 5). Beatitude has a communal dimension or none at all.

For Dante this vision of truth constitutes the crown of his journey through Hell, Purgatory, and Paradise. At the end of that journey he is gratuitously given the vision of man in the center of the rose, irrevocably bound into the life of the Trinity through the redemptive Incarnation of the eternal Logos. The Incarnation of the Second Person of the Trinity redeems man from the bonds of time and his own finite condition tending toward isolation. The impact of this revelation on Dante is staggering: the omega-point for man is everlasting union, through the incarnate Word, with "that Love which moves the sun and the other stars." The union is effected for the individual by incorporation into the divinity of the Word through a union in love with the Word incarnate in history. This union is dimensional, encompassing all of humankind which the Word died to redeem. In Dante's image of the multifoliate rose, each person is united with his neighbor in their common union with the Trinity at the center.

Eliot is, characteristically, restrained in his expression of this mysterious granting of experiential knowledge from outside the realm of human experience, and which forms the content of all mystical literature. His clearest statement occurs in the fifth section of "The Dry Salvages." Man's redemption from time will not result from his probing past and future for the meaning of life. It lies rather in his recognition and grasp of that moment of intrusion from beyond his own resources which carries with it the gift of understanding.

> Men's curiosity searches past and future
> And clings to that dimension. But to apprehend
> The point of intersection of the timeless
> With time, is an occupation for the saint–
> No occupation either, but something given
> And taken, in a lifetime's death in love,
> Ardour and selflessness and self-surrender.

The apprehension, though gratuitous, is given totally only to the saint, the one who loves totally, who lives on that costly level of awareness Krishna refers to in part 3 of "The Dry Salvages," where "The time of death is every moment." Throughout his poetry Eliot has paradoxically yoked together birth and death in the traditional Christian sense. The spiritually dead in *The Waste Land* must truly die to self and be aligned with Christ's death if they are to be given new life:

He who was living is now dead
We who were living are now dying
With a little patience.

Musing on the Incarnation, the old Magus asks, ". . . were we led all that way for / Birth or death? . . . This Birth was / Hard and bitter agony for us, like Death, our death." The protagonist of "Ash Wednesday" cheerfully undergoes dissembling from the three white leopards and claims that it is this surrender which recovers his hitherto unredeemed humanity. He asks the lady to "Pray for us sinners now and at the hour of our death." In "Animula" the entreaty is the same, though the word is reversed: "Pray for us now and at the hour of our birth." For the simple soul—"Irresolute and selfish, misshapen, lame"—life is a form of death. Animula comes to life only after sacramental union attained at the point of death: "Living first in the silence after the viaticum." For Eliot one state mystically contains the other: "In my end is my beginning" ("East Coker" 5).

In keeping with this tradition, Eliot in the sestina section of "The Dry Salvages," part 2, refers to the time of death as "The hardly, barely prayable / Prayer of the one Annunciation." That expression of surrender at the Annunciation made possible in time the Incarnation, the inbreak of divinity on man, of eternity on time. Eliot goes on in part 5 to describe by analogy the intermittent experience of the ordinary man, the nonsaint, in regard to these penetrations of vision:

For most of us, there is only the unattended
Moment, the moment in and out of time,
The distraction fit, lost in a shaft of sunlight,
The wild thyme unseen, or the winter lightning
Or the waterfall, or music heard so deeply
That it is not heard at all, but you are the music
While the music lasts.

These moments are given but not always apprehended. They are actually indicative of something that transcends them. To follow the moment of vision to its terminal significance demands a kind of readiness or basic orientation, a kind of apprenticeship of the spirit:

These are only hints and guesses,
Hints followed by guesses; and the rest
Is prayer, observance, discipline, thought and action.

The real revelation of man's ultimate meaning is for Eliot, as for Dante, the redemptive Incarnation. Every momentary and partial insight into the meaning of life and the place of man is a spark or shadow from that ultimate revelation:

> The hint half guessed, the gift half understood, is Incarnation.
> Here the impossible union
> Of spheres of existence is actual,
> Here the past and future
> Are conquered, and reconciled. . . .

Incarnation, for Eliot, is the reconciliation of opposites. He sees in the union of God and man the promise of the resolution of discordant time, place, and action. Insofar as one participates in this union of reconciliation, is he saved from the isolated selfhood which the women of Canterbury perceive as hell:

> Emptiness, absence, separation from God;
> The horror of the effortless journey to the empty land
> Which is no land, only emptiness, absence, the Void,
> Where those who were men can no longer turn the mind
> To distraction, delusion, escape into dream, pretence,
> Where the soul is no longer deceived, for there are no objects, no tones,
> No colours, no forms to distract, to divert the soul
> From seeing itself, foully united forever, nothing with nothing,
> Not what we call death, but what beyond death is not death,
> We fear, we fear.
>
> [*Murder in the Cathedral* 2]

The fact that *Murder in the Cathedral* is contemporary with the beginnings of *Four Quartets*[2] gives some indication of Eliot's preoccupation at this time with the idea of isolation and communion as damnation and beatitude.

The one can be summed up as conscious isolation. The soul sees itself united with nothing. In a state of beatitude the soul perceives itself united to ultimate love. The knowledge in either case is experiential, not speculative. But an experiential knowledge of infinite love in the finite person is something which "flesh cannot endure" ("Burnt Norton" 2). It can come only in flashes of insight which one does not always understand at the time but which time itself can deliver to one's understanding:

> We had the experience but missed the meaning,
> And approach to the meaning restores the experience
> In a different form, beyond any meaning
> We can assign to happiness.
>
> ["The Dry Salvages" 2]

Only through the maturity that comes from fidelity in a sustained effort to understand life can that understanding be conferred.

One sees in *Four Quartets* a progression in the protagonist's understanding and experience of the meaning of time and life. And in each case the lyric of the fourth movement distills that experience in its most complete form. "Burnt Norton" is riddled with flashes of beauty not quite apprehended. They are hints of the sheer loveliness and transforming significance of an incarnational experience not yet seen as incarnational. These flashes are embodied in images of the garden and the laughter of children: the world of primal innocence in which birds give commands and adults obey. In speculation on this world the protagonist suggests the possibility that

> Time past and time future
> What might have been and what has been
> Point to one end, which is always present.

In the incarnational experience itself all passing time is contained in the eternal "now." But this is reality in its fullness, and "human kind / Cannot bear very much reality." In looking at things as they are existentially in all their imperfection, the poet sees poor material for transformation. It is necessary to "Descend lower . . . / Into the world of perpetual solitude," a state of "Internal darkness, deprivation / And destitution" where human desires are purified. The only way to attain "The inner freedom from the practical desire" ("Burnt Norton" 2) is to lose oneself through denial of appetite. To move with the world in appetency is mechanical and merely a succession of meaningless events.

Immediately after this insight is reached, we have the lyric "Time and the bell have buried the day," which points ultimately to "The still point of the turning world." In the contrast of the world moving "In appetency, on its metalled ways" in part 3 and this point of stillness inhabited by the kingfisher, one is reminded of the punning lines in "Ash Wednesday" 5: "Against the Word the unstilled world still whirled / About the center of the silent Word." The still point has a special meaning to Eliot. The lyric of "Burnt Norton" is indeed incarnational. The paradox of birth and death, embodied in its deliberately ambiguous images, will become more explicit as the quartets proceed.

Part 5 explores the deeper significance of the moment of stillness where "all is always now." The last section apparently begins in a low-keyed, muted speculation about words. But words are here a paradigm of the Logos incarnated. This is surely confirmed by Eliot's reference a few lines farther on in the same section to the Word in the desert attacked by voices of temptation. The last paragraph of "Burnt Norton" recapitulates the material of the entire poem. Time, desire, and love are placed in relation to the necessary limitation of their true perception by finite creatures. Yet in spite of human limitations their true significance is revealed in sudden surprises like a shaft of sunlight and children's voices in the foliage. One must be alert to apprehend these unsignalled moments: "Quick now, here, now always." The last word is crucial. It indicates that the eternal is always there ready to break into time. By comparison with such moments ordinary routine is of no meaning: "Ridiculous the waste sad time / Stretching before and after."

"Burnt Norton" introduces the ideas to be developed and clarified through the progression of the quartets. Of the four it is the most obscure, and functionally so. The idea of the transcendent moment which redeems time is not an easy concept to grasp, far less communicate. Eliot here speculates about a strange perception imposing itself from something experienced but not quite understood. The lyric of part 4, with its ambiguous images of death and life, movement and stillness, embodies the uncertainties of the whole quartet. Yet it resolves implicitly these very uncertainties in its remarkable structure. The two interrogative statements are enclosed by opening and closing declarative statements, the first of which dismisses the images of sequential time while the other points to the stillness of the center, the eternally present light at the heart of temporal experience. The resolution reached with "The crowned knot of fire" closing the last quartet is implicit in the close of this lyric section of the first. The only place in "Burnt Norton" that explicitly states this ultimate solution is part 4. The lyric gathers all the questions and ghosts of answers, and distills them into a resolution.

Even though "Burnt Norton" speculates on an experience not quite grasped, the poem faces up to the cost required of one who would comprehend that elusive experience. The lyric comes in the poem immediately after the insight is reached concerning the need for "Internal darkness, deprivation," the need for self-abnegation and purgation of appetite in order to attain the condition of stillness at the heart of light.

In each of the quartets this pattern is maintained, each becoming more specific in the demands imposed from the insight granted. The second quartet in general moves more into the idea of suffering involved in the incarnational experience. But it also points to the integration and union possible only through this diminishment of the unredeemed self. As the mediator Christ was introduced in the "Burnt Norton" lyric masked in the symbol of kingfisher, he is explicitly brought into "East Coker" in the Passion lyric as the "wounded surgeon." Once again the lyric follows immediately upon a call to negation. In a paraphrase from St. John of the Cross's sketch of Mt. Carmel,[3] Eliot points the way to fullness and well-being through the path of ignorance and dispossession, a total state of spiritual "negative capability." The passage is much more explicit than its parallel in "Burnt Norton" 3.

It is worth noting some of the fine points of Eliot's selection of sources. Biblically Elijah's Mt. Carmel is the place of a true revelation of the personal God Yahweh and his ascendancy over the prophets of Baal (1 Kings 18). John of the Cross chose the ascent of this mountain as the metaphor for the way of true abnegation which is not an end in itself, but a preparation for union with a personal God. It is such a God who, in Eliot, hovers over the life of man, ready to overtake him with a love which he describes as "the absolute paternal care / That will not leave us, but prevents us everywhere." "East Coker" deals with the costliness of such a union. The fourth-part lyric, which focuses on the Passion and the Eucharist, emphasizes the fact that self-knowledge is the prerequisite for the pursuit of union with Christ through purgation of personal sin. Only through realization of one's distance from God can one bridge the gap through a eucharistic union with Christ as mediator and vicarious victim. Unlike "Burnt Norton" "East Coker" ends with a consideration of that moment not as

> . . . the intense moment
> Isolated, with no before and after,
> But a lifetime burning in every moment. . . .

In the second movement of "East Coker" Eliot speaks of the folly of those who have come through life in fear of being possessed, "Of belonging to another, or to others, or to God." He closes the quartet with the conclusion that

> We must be still and still moving
> Into another intensity
> For further union, a deeper communion
> Through the dark cold and the empty desolation.

Death is seen as "life's high meed," the final moment where the individual is redeemed from sequential time and caught up into the still center of eternal presence: "In my end is my beginning." The closing image of "East Coker" is one of the sea: "The wave cry, the wind cry, the vast water / Of the petrel and the porpoise." It fittingly introduces the material of "The Dry Salvages," concerned with its "calamitous annunication" of total diminishment, that moment which, if lived rightly, reveals itself to be the moment of perfect fulfillment because it is the moment of perfect union of the finite will with the infinite.

The third quartet is the most specifically incarnational of the four and in turn moves deeper into the role of suffering and death in the life of the individual. But here death is seen as a particular and universal call constituting the moment of truth in the life of a person. That moment is seen as annunciation, and Eliot unmistakably yokes this with the Annunciation signalling the Incarnation. The incredible complication in the layers of meaning, so hard to paraphrase, is told in a notably lucid style in this third quartet. In the sestina section Eliot deals with the double idea of physical death ("The calamitous annunciation"), and with death-to-self:

> Years of living among the breakage
> Of what was believed in as the most reliable–
> And therefore the fittest for renunciation.

Both these deaths point to one end always present as the moment of grace and insight: "Only the hardly, barely prayable, / Prayer of the one Annunciation." This is a much more explicit handling of incarnation than either the kingfisher hint of "Burnt Norton" or the Good Friday meditation of "East Coker." The successive pattern of each emerging quartet is like a series of concentric circles, each one an increment from the first splash of a pebble. Each depends on the speculations and insights of the one preceding in order to come to its own expansion and deepening of those thoughts.

Eliot weaves together most intricately the ideas put forth in the earlier quartets while concentrating more and more on the significance of the timeless moment to the individual person. With the Krishna section of part 3 he speaks of a dimension of consciousness transcending the limits of self-orientation. This passage is a suitable preparation for the lyric of part 4, a prayer to the Virgin of the Annunciation to intercede for those in their "last annunciation," those who have gone beyond the reach of "the sea bell's / Perpetual angelus." It is crucial that the angelus is perpetual. The moment in the rose garden ("Burnt Norton" 2) and the moment "When here and now cease to matter" ("East Coker" 5) are coming closer together in a realization that the moment of annunciation, the moment of possibility, is always present. It is so because the Word has become immanent through the consent of one individual. It is ultimately Mary who leads Dante to the center of the rose.

The intercessory nature of the lyric emphasizes the communal aspect of reaching this point of completion. This lyric distills all that went before and holds incipiently what is to emerge in part 5: a direct meditation on and attempt to define the significance of the Incarnation for the created world and for the life of man and of individual men. It is of the utmost significance that "The Dry Salvages," which contains the most explicit statement of the Incarnation, is the only one of the quartets that makes no mention in part 5 of the artist's struggle with words and meanings. It is not concerned with words as symbols and metaphors, but deals directly with the reality of the Word incarnate in the world. The theme, stated as it is, incorporates all the related material of "Burnt Norton" and "East Coker," and prepares for the conclusion of "Little Gidding."

The last quartet concentrates on an exploration of the understanding reached in "The Dry Salvages." The exploration stretches into the past and future and points to the mysterious present: "Here, the intersection of the timeless moment / Is England and nowhere. Never and always." The doctrine of the Incarnation presented in "The Dry Salvages" receives more concrete application to life and history in "Little Gidding." The fourth quartet explicitly deals with prayer and with the pentecostal dimension of a life of awareness and union with the divine. The role of prayer, introduced in the lyric of "The Dry Salvages," is concentrated upon in "Little Gidding." Eliot deliberately chooses for his setting a place "where prayer has been valid." Here the "dumb spirit" is stirred by "pentecostal fire / In the dark time of the year."

The poem recapitulates the meaning of past time in the life of the individual and the life of man in history. For the individual, confrontation with the past involves a painful reenactment of past deeds. Eliot gives this reenactment powerful expression in the terza rima encounter with the old master in part 3. The most penetrating form of self-evaluation is reached only in those moments of truth bordering on death:

> And last, the rending pain of re-enactment
>   Of all that you have done, and been; the shame
>   Of motives late revealed, and the awareness
> Of things ill done and done to others' harm
>   Which once you took for exercise of virtue.

The only way to restore oneself from such a chain of wrongdoing is through the refining fire of purgation. But purgation here is subtle and very refined indeed. It pierces the marrow with its discrimination of motive. It differentiates between attachment, detachment, and indifference as between life and death. Knowledge of sin can be salvific, however, because it can lead to reliance on grace which is outside of oneself. In "Little Gidding" "Sin is Behovely," for it is the material on which forgiveness works. The expression of Juliana of Norwich used here parallels the *O felix culpa* of the Christian paschal liturgy:

> All manner of thing shall be well
> By the purification of the motive
> In the ground of our beseeching.

The subjects of sin and transforming grace are brought together. Salvation comes through the action of grace which purifies the motive, thus orienting the person away from isolation bringing spiritual death, and toward union conferring life. Krishna's message in "The Dry Salvages" is given more definite application here. It is necessary that "the ground of our beseeching" become aligned with the ground of our being. Otherwise radical disorientation of the self will take place and the person will be destroyed.

Only after the presentation of this insight does Eliot confront us with the pentecostal lyric and its radical choice:

> The only hope, or else despair–
> Lies in the choice of pyre or pyre–
> To be redeemed from fire by fire.

The thoughts that ensue from confrontation with the necessity of radical choice are peaceful and conciliatory. Words can once again be dealt with as symbols, but symbols whose significance is now understood because of the intervention of the Logos passage in "The Dry Salvages." The last movement of "Little Gidding" recapitulates all the images of incarnational experience from the earlier quartets: the children's voices, the end as beginning, the stillness between two waves of the sea. The moment is always there, eternally present and immanent. To apprehend it is the condition of the saint: "A condition of complete simplicity / (Costing not less than everything)." When this condition is reached, all things shall be well indeed. Eliot closes with a variation on Dante's rose–a variation which emphasizes his own particular insights. Purgation and love, the fire and the rose, are one. The image of reconciliation is deep.

Each of the fourth section lyrics distills the essence of the quartet in which it occurs. Lifted out and juxtaposed, the lyrics form a sequence in which is embodied the essential progression of ideas for the entire four. "Time and the bell" presents us with insights not quite understood, hints and guesses not quite apprehended, but truly part of experience and pointing to an end outside themselves. Such experience leads the poet to meditate on its possible meaning. "The wounded surgeon" lyric shapes this insight into an overtly Christian meditation on the Passion of Christ and man's incorporation into that redemptive act through participation in the Eucharist. The Marian lyric of "The Dry Salvages" is cast in the form of a prayer at the time of one's personal annunciation. In view of the significance of the Virgin in Dante and in Christian tradition, the lyric of the third quartet is a definite move toward the incorporation hinted by the kingfisher's wing in "Burnt Norton" and pondered in the eucharistic meditation of "East Coker." To petition the Virgin of the Annunciation is to pray that the Incarnation be made efficacious in one's own life.

It is worthwhile considering here the traditional prayer which ends the angelus:

> Pour forth, we beseech thee, O Lord, thy grace into our hearts; that we, to whom the incarnation of Christ, thy son, was made known by the message of an angel, may by his passion and cross be brought to the glory of his resurrection, through the same Jesus Christ our Lord. Amen. (Roman Missal)

This is the thrust of the entire *Four Quartets.* The final direction for the attainment of such a goal is presented in the pentecostal lyric of "Little Gidding." The preceding lyrics show increasing insight into the human condition and the need "For a further union, a deeper communion" with others and with God. Part 4 of "Little Gidding" directs one to the alternatives of damnation or beatitude through purgation of whatever constitutes a barrier to union. The choice is stark and the lyric is simple and profound. Beatitude is communal; community is costly. Acceptance of a radical purgation of selfishness and indifference leads to attainment of the beatitude of union; for purgation is prompted by love, "the unfamiliar Name" behind the suffering involved in such a purification. The fire and the rose are perceived as one through "the drawing of this Love and the voice of this Calling."

The fourth movement lyrics are indeed remarkable in their individual excellence and in the way Eliot uses the traditional economy of lyric power to embody the central ideas of his *Four Quartets.* In four short passages of heightened emotion and intensity, Eliot telescopes the content of each quartet. In sequence the lyrics telescope the entire progression of the four through the presentation of an experiential knowledge evolving from hints and guesses to the point of radical choice. Such use of the lyric shows consummate skill. Eliot employs the traditional qualities of the lyric not only as separate pieces, but even more notably as distillations of longer poems and as a sequential summation of the entire series. It is a very original and effective use of the power proper to the lyric.

CHAPTER SIX

A FINAL APPRAISAL

Leonard Unger in 1965 referred to Eliot as "contemporary." In this evaluation he included the later works, not just "The Love Song of J. Alfred Prufrock," *The Waste Land,* and "The Hollow Men."[1] M. H. Abrams held to this appraisal in 1971 when he maintained that "even after a quarter-century, T. S. Eliot's *Four Quartets* has not lost its status as a strikingly 'modern' poem. . . ."[2] A common tendency among readers, however, is to write off *Four Quartets* as an unfortunate poetic aberration in which a good poet peters out to no good end under the unsavory influence of his religious sensibility. Quite the opposite is true. The quartets are the logical outcome of his poetic career. Eliot is no mean poet and consistently shows critical acumen in self-evaluation. He considered *Four Quartets* his best work. It seems that more consideration could be given to his own judgment on this point without compromising one's critical integrity.

Undoubtedly one of the problems with *Four Quartets* is the subject matter. Perhaps the orthodox Christianity to which they give expression is unsympathetic to the modern reader.[3] Ironically Eliot, by giving this traditional subject matter new expression, has turned away just as many orthodox readers by his manner as he has the nonreligious readers by his subject. Eliot is aware of the risks inherent in his subject and manner of expression: "To feel things in one's own way, however intensely, is likely to look like frigidity to those who can only feel in accepted ways."[4] Such a problem would in no way determine Eliot's choice. His is the classical Charybdis-Scylla dilemma which inheres in the situation itself. The alternative would be not to write at all. Long before the writing of *Four Quartets* Eliot was "occupied with the struggle—which alone constitutes life for a poet—to transmute his personal and private agonies into something rich and strange, something universal and impersonal" (*SE,* p. 117). It remains true that the poet has only his own experiences to go on. If the subject matter is uncongenial to a great number of people, so much the worse for reaching a large audience if that is his intention. For Eliot it is a matter of personal development in both method and subject.

In 1941, when he was still writing the quartets, Eliot noted the relation of form and subject in the development of Rudyard Kipling. During the various periods of Kipling's life when his attention was absorbed by different interests, his verse mirrors these changes in rhythm, imagery, and form. There is a "compulsion to find, in every new poem as in his earliest, the right form for feelings over the development of which he has, as a poet, no control" (*PP,* p. 276). One can trace a similar personal and stylistic development in Eliot from "The Love Song of J. Alfred Prufrock" to *Four Quartets.* It is worth noting that Eliot stands by his later work unequivocally. He makes no apology for *Four Quartets.* In the Donald Hall interview already cited, he is forthrightly anxious that these poems should be understood in all their religious meaning. There are no smokescreens, no gargoyles such as "Hakagawa bowing among the Titians," to make the reader unsure about the poet's attitude toward what he portrays. In the quartets he seems sure of himself and has no need for the protection of obscurity. The poems are, in part, clear expositions of certain theological attitudes toward reality. Woven into the philosophical fabric is the intense force of lyrical expression used to fix, to capture definitively, to concretize the elusive abstractions. This is the method of mystical literature, most notably exemplified by St. John of the Cross, the sixteenth-century Spanish Carmelite whom Eliot read and paraphrased in his own work. Of course John wrote the lyrics for their own sake. Only when asked for exposition of these short poems did he write his long prose commentaries, including the combined works under the titles of the original lyrics: *The Dark Night of the Soul, The Living Flame of Love,* etc. Eliot uses a somewhat reverse process. In his more proselike passages he expounds what he perceives regarding certain observed truths. Then he puts flesh on the abstractions by letting them take form in lyric expression. John's prose was an expansion of a very distilled lyric form; Eliot's lyrics are a distillation of more leisurely philosophical speculations in verse.

To appreciate *Four Quartets* one need not believe in what Eliot so earnestly expounds, any more than one must believe in the communion of saints in order to appreciate Dante's tremendously felicitous metaphor of the rose rising out of an ocean of light. All one needs is "that willing suspension of disbelief . . . which constitutes poetic faith" that has been afforded to poets by readers in all centuries. There seems at present, however, a great resistance to this kind of liberalism in the reading of poetry. To complain about the late poetry of Eliot because it does not say the same things in the same way as his early poetry is unproductive. Eliot has said: "As a man grows older, he may turn to new subject-matter, or he may treat the same material in a different way; as we age we both live in a different world, and become different men in the same world" (*PP,* p. 276). Eliot's poetry is of a piece, woven from beginning to end with the same concerns. But it is evolutionary. If Apeneck Sweeney and flat-footed Doris are not center stage, their predicament is still there–no longer as the object of observation merely, or of condemnation and disgust, but of compassion, a large comprehensiveness of vision which accepts the human condition as a given, and tries to transform its reality by a response to divine grace.

This expansion of vision is for Eliot a matter of art as well as life. Thus Eliot's art changes with different stages of his life. It is as John of the Cross expressed it: " . . . when a person is learning new details about his art or trade, he must work in darkness and not with what he already knows. If he refuses to lay aside his former knowledge, he will never make any further progress."[5] Eliot in *Four Quartets* is liberated from his early poetry without repudiating it. He thus liberates himself from a possible pose which that poetry might have inflicted upon him. Eliot is liberated, not in the sense of turning his back on his early poems, but rather in the sense of gathering them up and going beyond them in form and in substance. A careful look at *Four Quartets* will verify their various excellences, not the least of which is Eliot's mastery of the lyric genre and his masterful handling of lyric forms within a longer poem of decidedly philosophical tone. Far from showing the debilitation of a "worn-out poetical fashion," such performance shows lively creativity in the adaptation of a traditional form. *Four Quartets* is a "really new" work of art in the sense Eliot describes in "Tradition and the Individual Talent" (*SE,* pp. 3–11). It takes the best aspects of an ancient tradition, the lyric, and turns them to a truly innovative use.

In estimating the contributions of various innovators among the twentieth-century poets, Mark Van Doren notes that "T. S. Eliot experimented, to be sure, with stanzas and free verse; it is quite important that he did so; but it is still more important that he restored to poetry the stuff of theology, long absent and all but lost."[6] Restoring to poetry the stuff of theology is a formidable accomplishment, but Eliot has also restored the stuff of lyricism to philosophical poetry, thus imbuing it with a disciplined precision as well as an emotional intensity. From beginning to end Eliot employs techniques of lyricism to convey his most profound philosophical and theological insights. As he develops from an ethical poet to a religious poet, Eliot's religious sensibility becomes more and more refined, and the vehicle of its expression, his poetry, more and more accomplished in lyrical skill. In the process of finding the right mode of expression for his religious evolution, Eliot has effected some of the most original uses of the oldest poetic genre, the lyric.

In a century when poetry has become highly cerebral, and the sound-structures which convey the meaning of that poetry consequently more complex, it is significant that one of the most overtly intellectual poets of the age would turn to the most uncerebral form in literary history to find body for his ideas. Perhaps it is the only way. Indeed, it would seem so, for the result is a perfect coalition of form and meaning.

We have seen how Eliot uses lyric techniques to maintain the tension between the romantic and the cynical within the personality of J. Alfred Prufrock, thus heightening the emotional tone of a nonlyrical poem. Throughout the early poetry, and continuing into *Four Quartets,* a definite correspondence is maintained between Eliot's desire to convey intense emotional experience and his use of lyricism in the various poems. In *The Waste Land*—a poem full of encounters with no communication—all hints, all intimations of real human value through love are effected by Eliot's careful use of lyrical devices and allusions.

Totally different is the pervasive, trancelike lyricism of "The Hollow Men" which exemplifies the spiritual torpor of those who have lost the good of both intellect and will. Yet Eliot can use the equally pervasive lyricism of "Ash Wednesday" to convey the higher dream of the human spirit in pursuit of God. The difference is one of craftsmanship, not accident. In "Ash Wednesday" Eliot uses liturgical and paraliturgical allusion as a shaping force to what would otherwise seem a nebulous meditation. The result demonstrates a powerful lyric competence.

We see in the Eliot corpus a direct relationship between religious conviction and the use of lyricism. This is not surprising in view of the fact that religious ideas are what carry the strongest emotional force in Eliot's poetry. Throughout his criticism—and it has been pointed out continually in this study—Eliot has emphasized the necessity of religious sensibility to religious belief: "The trouble of the modern age is not merely the inability to believe certain things about God and man . . . , but the inability to *feel* towards God and man. . . ."[7] There is in religion an emotional factor that eludes philosophical categorization. Eliot's lyricism becomes a vehicle for his theology—a theology of salvation through union and reconciliation, the realization "Of belonging to another, or to others, or to God" ("East Coker" 3).

In Eliot's hands the lyric becomes a lodestone of judgment on the selfish irresponsibility of isolation. "La Figlia che Piange" condemns the cold objectivity of the aesthete in the face of human desertion and heartbreak;

"Eyes that last I saw in tears" exposes the barren spiritual landscape of the disembodied soul who failed to respond to love and is, through his affective impotence of will, damned to an eternity of inefficacious self-evaluation. These lyrics are two outstanding examples because of their brevity and self-containment, but the same functional lyricism intensifies the moral judgments made on the man in the hyacinth garden, Gerontion, the rich woman in "A Game of Chess," the typist and the clerk in "The Fire Sermon."

As Eliot comes to the *Ariel Poems* and "Ash Wednesday," his theology of salvation moves in a direction more positive, and we see emerging the sacramentality of time and place as mediators of eschatological values. In "Marina" he refers to "this grace dissolved in place"; in "Ash Wednesday" he speaks of "This . . . time of tension between dying and birth." Eliot is increasingly caught up in a contemplation of the significance of time and place to the life of the individual and his response to reality. It is only here and now that mediate the eternal present and the eternal presence immanent in the world through the Incarnation, but entering into each individual's life unannounced in moments of rare illumination that demand a response. The quality of one's awareness of and response to the present moment determines his ultimate value:

> At the moment which is not of action or inaction
> You can receive this: "on whatever sphere of being
> The mind of a man may be intent
> At the time of death"—that is the one action
> (And the time of death is every moment)
> Which shall fructify in the lives of others. . . .
> ["The Dry Salvages" 3]

Eliot, like Dante, emphasizes both the communal and the gratuitous dimensions of salvation through his use of the intercessory figure: the lost daughter of "Marina," the veiled sister of "Ash Wednesday."

By *Four Quartets* the image becomes clearly archetypal as Mary, the Virgin of the Annunciation, bringing Christ into the world of human history and interceding with him on behalf of humankind facing the calamitous annunciation of temporal dissolution. The sense of community is signalled by other allusions as well. The compound ghost of an old master, those who died on the scaffold during a civil strife long past, those who die at sea, Krishna on the field of battle, the lost children in the foliage, the rustic dancers leaping through the flames—all are united in a common humanity with a common call to final union. All have something salvific to communicate to the present generation.

In sequence the fourth-section lyrics of *Four Quartets* epitomize the universal and individual experience of salvation. The sudden illuminations of "Burnt Norton" in "Time and the bell" are mediated through earthly things—flowers, vines, birds, trees—and indicate the still point of eternity in the symbolic action of the kingfisher. Meaning emerges as paradox in the "wounded surgeon" meditation of "East Coker" on the Passion and the Eucharist and on what it means to experience one's own need for redemption. The Marian lyric of "The Dry Salvages" places the individual in an attitude of prayer to the Virgin Mother to intercede for all of humankind, men and women, past and present. The communal need for salvation is stressed in this lyric and in the pentecostal message of "Little Gidding" 4, where we are directed toward discernment and choice in the radical core of the human will made perfect by love.

It is no strange world that emerges in *Four Quartets,* but our world of nature, benevolent and terrifying; of human brothers and sisters to whom one is accountable, and who influence one's life in time; of events natural and unnatural, good and evil, which we must somehow not only get through, but learn to use as sacramental encounters with love, the "unfamiliar Name" behind all our moments of annunciation. The world of *Four Quartets* is familiar in a way that those of "Ash Wednesday" and "Marina" are not. By the time of *Four Quartets* Eliot has come to terms with his religious conversion. Religious conversion has evolved into religious experience of a more pervasive and leavening kind in which

> The moment of the rose and the moment of the yew-tree
> Are of equal duration.
> . . . for history is a pattern
> Of timeless moments.
> . . . .
> History is now and England.
> With the drawing of this Love and voice of this Calling.
> ["Little Gidding" 5]

The purpose of all human life is union:

> We must be still and still moving
> Into another intensity
> For a further union, a deeper communion. . . .
> ["East Coker" 5]

We see these themes running through the fabric of Eliot's poetry. They form a theology imbued with intensity of feeling because it is a theology of relationship, of communion. It is an eminently reasonable aspiration of humankind belonging to a long tradition which includes the great mystics of Western thought. But the theology of union and its implications go beyond unaided reasonableness. It requires, according to Eliot, "A condition of complete simplicity / (Costing not less than everything.)" To put into words this dawning realization Eliot has continually resorted to lyric expression, and has developed his lyric technique into lyric mastery in the process of perfecting that expression.

In the early poems we catch glimpses and hints of these insights—what it really means to be in relation or not in relation to others. In the first religious poetry of the late 1920s and early 1930s (*Ariel Poems* and "Ash Wednesday"), we see a haunting, ecstatic expression of a newly realized understanding of the self in relation to God and others. In *Four Quartets* we see the lyrical distillation of all his cumulative theological understanding. The lyrics compress the salvation history of the individual and of humankind. Throughout his career Eliot has used lyricism as the vehicle for this religious sensibility and theological perception. As the perception runs clearer, so does the poetry. The lyrics of *Four Quartets* are among the most functionally original in twentieth-century poetry, and are of an artistic quality not surpassed.

Just as Mark Van Doren has pointed out Eliot's contribution in restoring to twentieth-century poetry the stuff of theology, so Russell Kirk has cited Eliot's restoration to his age of the moral imagination.[8] Certainly he holds a prominent and sure place in the history of twentieth-century thought. To a milieu which he perceived as a kind of spiritual wasteland in 1922, T. S. Eliot gradually restored over a period of some forty years not only a moral awareness but the springs of a religious sensibility as well. And it is in the perfecting of his mastery in the lyric form that these restorations are most fully and effectively embodied.

APPENDIX

SKETCH OF MT. CARMEL BY ST. JOHN OF THE CROSS

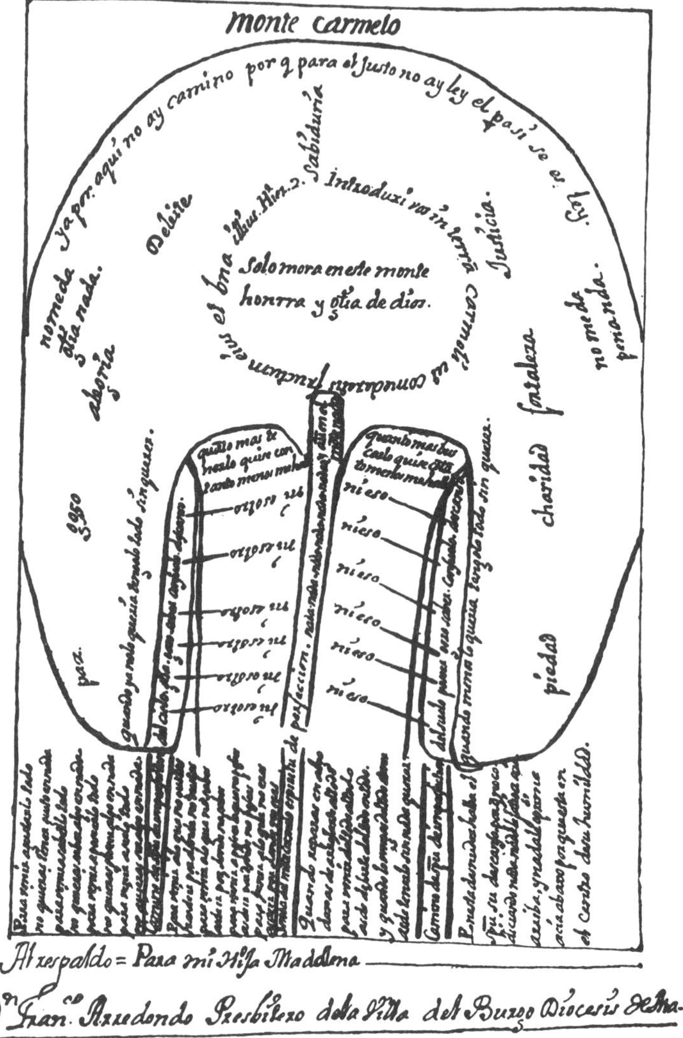

From *The Collected Works of St. John of the Cross* (Institute of Carmelite Studies Publications, 1974), pp. 66–7.

ENGLISH TRANSLATION OF TERMS USED IN ST. JOHN'S ORIGINAL DRAWING

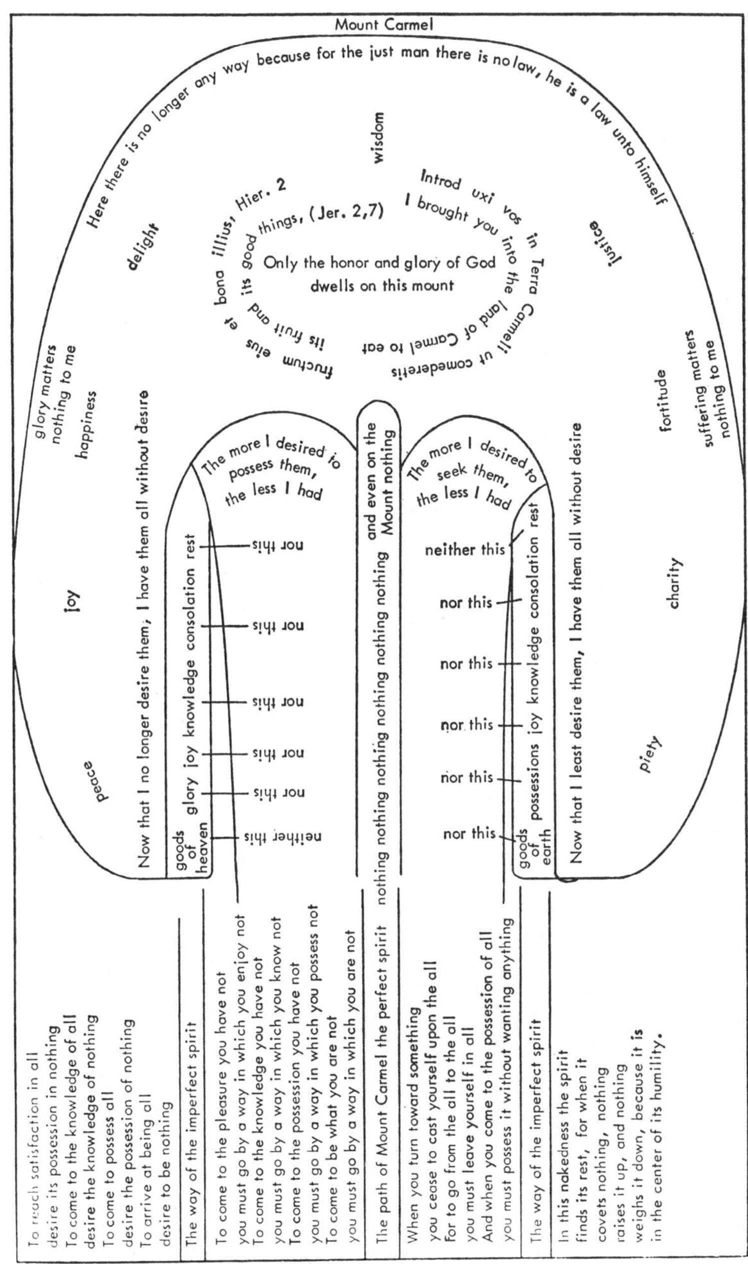

NOTES

1. THE THEORY OF THE LYRIC

1. *The Achievement of T. S. Eliot.*
2. *The Art of T. S. Eliot.* A particularly fine discussion of Eliot's poetry is Genesius Jones's *Approach to the Purpose: A Study of the Poetry of T. S. Eliot* (Hodder and Stoughton, 1964).
3. Too many citations would have to be given for an adequate idea of how frequently Eliot reiterates this point. For a typical passage cf. *UP,* p. 83.
4. Introduction, Knight, p. xx.
5. Ibid., p. xvii.
6. *SE,* p. 4.
7. Olson, "An Outline . . . , " pp. 546–66. Cf. also Olson, *Aristotle's Poetics.*
8. Appleton, *American Lyric Poems,* 1964.
9. This matter of personal expression has always been a needless point of contention in the consideration of lyric verse. Eliot himself finds it a stumbling block for lyric definition. Cf. p. 7.
10. *"On the Morning of Christ's Nativity" by J. Milton, for 3 (or 2) soloists, chorus, semichorus and orchestra* (London: Stainer and Bell, 1928).
11. *Epithalamion, a cantata for baritone solo, chorus, and small orchestra. Based on the masque, "The Bridal Day."* Words by E. Spenser (London: Oxford University Press, 1957).
12. "Rudyard Kipling," *PP,* pp. 293–94.
13. "The Three Voices of Poetry," pp. 105–6.
14. "In Memoriam," p. 289.
15. "What Is Minor Poetry?" p. 43.
16. "Goethe as the Sage," p. 264.
17. "Yeats," pp. 303–4.
18. In his essay "The Three Voices" cited above, Eliot makes one specific generic exception regarding what he classifies as poetry of the first voice: "The voice of the poet talking to himself or to nobody" (p. 96). "I must make the point that this poetry is not necessarily what we call loosely

'lyrical poetry' " (p. 105). "I should prefer to say 'meditative verse' " (p. 106).
19. "The Function of Criticism," p. 19.
20. "Johnson as Critic and Poet," pp. 194, 200, 215–16.
21. Introduction, Valéry, p. ix.

2. ELIOT'S DEVELOPMENT AS A LYRIC POET

1. "The Problems of the Shakespeare Sonnets," pp. 664, 666.
2. "The Three Voices of Poetry," p. 109.
3. "The Music of Poetry," p. 23.
4. *The Sacred Wood,* p. 169.
5. *The Hidden God,* pp. 68–97.
6. *The Poems of John Keats,* p. 206.
7. *The Poems of Tennyson,* p. 280.
8. Introduction, Pound, p. 9.
9. "The Music of Poetry," p. 30.
10. *The Achievement of T. S. Eliot,* p. 114.
11. "Milton II," p. 183.
12. "From Poe to Valéry," p. 332.
13. "Goethe as the Sage," p. 262.
14. "Johnson as Critic and Poet," pp. 190–91.
15. "Rudyard Kipling," p. 285.
16. "Dante," p. 228.
17. Introduction, Paul Valéry, *The Art of Poetry,* p. xiv.
18. *The Art of T. S. Eliot,* p. 102.
19. "The Music of Poetry," p. 22.
20. "What Is a Classic?" pp. 52–74; and "Virgil and the Christian World," pp. 135–48.

3. LYRICISM IN THE LONGER POEMS

1. This was first pointed out to me by Professor Giovanni Giovannini, now professor emeritus, The Catholic University of America.

2. Cf. "Dirge" (1) in T. S. Eliot, *The Waste Land: A Facsimile and Transcript of the Original Drafts Including the Annotations of Ezra Pound,* ed. Valerie Eliot (Harcourt Brace Jovanovich, 1971), p. [119].

3. No wonder Eliot deleted the short lyric "Eyes that last I saw in tears" from this poem. To have that ultimate encounter with its concomitant pain is not for the hollow men.

4. In [Edward] Elgar, *The Dream of Gerontius: An Oratorio for Mezzo-Soprano, Tenor and Bass Soli, Chrous and Orchestra. Poem by Cardinal Newman* (Novello and Co., 1900), pp. 159–61.

5. *Collected Works of St. John of the Cross,* pp. 69–70.

6. *The Cloud of Unknowing,* pp. 53–54.

7. In noting the particular beauty of the English Church in his essay "Lancelot Andrewes" (1926), Eliot nevertheless comments: "The English Church has no literary monument equal to that of Dante, no intellectual

monument equal to that of St. Thomas, no devotional monument equal to that of St. John of the Cross" (*SE,* p. 300).

8. "Second Thoughts about Humanism" (1928), *SE,* p. 433.

9. Donald Hall, "The Art of Poetry I: T. S. Eliot: An Interview," *Paris Review* 40 (spring, summer, 1959): 63.

10. Ibid.

11. Ibid., 63–64.

12. Ibid., 64.

13. Ibid., 63.

4. AN APPRAISAL OF THE LYRIC MOVEMENTS IN *FOUR QUARTETS*

1. From the cover of "T. S. Eliot Reads His *Four Quartets,*" Angel Recordings, 45012.

2. Eliot published "Burnt Norton" in 1936 in *Collected Poems.* "East Coker" (1940), "The Dry Salvages" (1941), and "Little Gidding" (1942) were all published in pamphlet form.

3. "Johnson as Critic and Poet," p. 203.

4. "The Social Function of Poetry," p. 15.

5. "Shakespeare and the Stoicism of Seneca," p. 115.

6. "The Metaphysical Poets," p. 246.

7. "Rudyard Kipling," p. 289.

8. "Dante," p. 214.

9. "Yeats," p. 302.

10. *Essays Ancient and Modern,* p. 133.

11. Introduction, Pound, pp. 17, 18.

12. "Goethe as the Sage," p. 263.

13. "John Dryden," p. 268.

14. *The Sacred Wood,* p. 17.

15. "The Social Function of Poetry," p. 12.

16. "Leçon de Valéry," p. 214.

17. "The Music of Poetry," p. 32.

18. To give the shortest example: Eliot uses "question" in the sense of *OED 5b,* to bring into question, make doubtful or insecure; or *6,* to investigate (a thing). The illustrations for *5b* are dated 1637 and 1643; those for *6* are from 1599–1633, 1655. Both *5b* and *6* are labelled *Obs., Rare.*

19. See, for example, Eliot's explanation of Donne's popularity in the twentieth century: "And we are not wholly fanciful in believing that he has, in the old sense of the word, 'prevented' us." "Donne in Our Time," p. 18.

20. "Johnson as Critic and Poet," p. 214.

21. This self-containment of each stanza was emphasized in the editions before 1963 by an indentation of the initial lines. This indentation was dropped in the jubilee edition probably because it was not needed to signal a unit already so structurally marked.

22. "Philip Massinger," p. 187.

23. Preface, *Anabasis,* p. 10.

24. "A Note on Richard Crashaw," p. 36.

25. "Swinburne as Poet," pp. 283, 284, 285.
26. "Philip Massinger," p. 185.
27. "Dante," p. 226.
28. "Reflections on Contemporary Poetry I," 119.
29. "The Author of the 'Burning Babe,' " p. 508.
30. Raymond Preston notes that Eliot considered Adam as "the ruined millionaire." Preston had thought it to be the Fallen Angel before conferring with the poet. Cf. *Four Quartets Rehearsed,* p. 35.
31. "Dante," p. 213.
32. "The Frontiers of Criticism," p. 118.
33. Introduction, Moore, p. xii.
34. "Rudyard Kipling," p. 275.
35. "Ben Jonson," p. 128.
36. Eliot has said: "The business of the poet is to be more conscious of his own language than other men, to be more sensitive to the feeling, more aware of the meaning of every word he uses, more aware of the history of the language and of every word he uses, than other men." Cf. "Ezra Pound," 337.
37. "Andrew Marvell," 808.
38. "Marianne Moore," 595.
39. *American Literature and the American Language,* p. 16.
40. "Rudyard Kipling," p. 278.
41. "The Music of Poetry," p. 30.
42. Introduction, Moore, p. xiii.
43. The interrogative could equally be construed as two separate sentences, the second one an ellipsis. The double punctuation warrants this, whereas the omitted verb repetition favors the above interpretation. Neither way affects the structure of meaning which comprises a unit within the interrogative sequence.
44. "The Music of Poetry," p. 20.
45. *George Herbert,* pp. 8, 31.
46. *The Art of Poetry,* p. xiv.
47. *George Herbert,* p. 33.
48. "Swinburne as Poet," pp. 82–83.
49. "Reflections on Vers Libre," 518–19.
50. Qui se' a noi meridïana face
di caritate, e giuso, intra i mortali,
se' di speranza fontana vivace.
[*Paradiso* 33.10–12]
51. Nel ventre tuo si racesse l'amore
per lo cui caldo nell' etterna pace
così è germinato questo fiore.
[*Paradiso* 33.7–9]
52. Introduction, Moore, p. xii.
53. Perhaps it is precisely *because* of this tradition with its burden of effeminate and sentimental overtones that Eliot moves in the other direction. Just as Dante by the virile prayer he puts into the mouth of St. Bernard dissociates that saint from the sentimental lyric cult of the Virgin traceable to him in the Middle Ages, Eliot by stripping a Marian lyric of its conventional trappings restores it to an emotional vigor.

54. Line 2 might be considered an exception, ending as it does on a stress. But while "those" constitutes the stressed beat of the split trochee "those" / "whose," it is, nevertheless, much lighter than the heavily stressed catalectic "ships" which immediately precedes it.
55. Introduction, *Pound,* p. viii.
56. Ibid., p. xi.
57. *For Lancelot Andrewes,* p. 134.
58. "Johnson as Critic and Poet," pp. 190, 193.
59. Introduction, *The Art of Poetry,* p. xvi.
60. "Milton I," p. 161.
61. "From Poe to Valéry," p. 332.
62. Introduction, Pound, p. 9.
63. "Donne in Our Time," pp. 16, 17.
64. "The Metaphysical Poets," p. 245.
65. *PP,* pp. 17–33.
66. Introduction, *Literary Essays of Ezra Pound,* p. xiii.

5. THE FUNCTION OF LYRICS IN *FOUR QUARTETS*

1. "From Poe to Valéry," p. 334.
2. "Burnt Norton" was begun with fragments left over from the writing of the play.
3. *Collected Works of St. John of the Cross,* p. 66. See appendix for the sketch and its translation, pp. 104–5.

6. A FINAL APPRAISAL

1. "T. S. Eliot, 1888–1965," pp. 408–10.
2. *Natural Supernaturalism,* p. 319.
3. Of course the religious and transcendental experiences which occupy Eliot in *Four Quartets* are part of Eastern as well as Western heritage, though his language is predominantly from the Western tradition.
4. Introduction, Moore, p. xi.
5. *Collected Works of St. John of the Cross,* pp. 365–66.
6. "The Possible Importance of Poetry," p. 23.
7. "The Social Function of Poetry," p. 15.
8. *Eliot and His Age.*

BIBLIOGRAPHY

T. S. ELIOT

After Strange Gods: A Primer of Modern Heresy. Harcourt, Brace, 1934.

American Literature and the American Language. Washington University Press, 1953.

"Andrew Marvell." *Nation and Athenaeum* 33 (1923): 809.

"The Author of 'The Burning Babe.' " *Times Literary Supplement* 1278 (29 Jan. 1926): 508.

"Ben Jonson" (1919). *Selected Essays.* Harcourt, Brace & World, 1960, pp. 127–39.

"The Borderline of Prose." *New Statesman* 9 (1917): 157–59.

Charles Whibley: A Memoir. Oxford University Press, 1931.

"A Commentary: That Poetry Is Made with Words." *New English Weekly* 15 (27 Apr. 1939): 27–28.

"Dante" (1929). *Selected Essays.* Harcourt, Brace & World, 1960, pp. 199–240.

"Deux Attitudes mystiques: Dante et Donne." *Le Roseau d'or: oeuvres et chroniques: Troisième Numero de Chroniques.* Librarie Plon, 1927, 149–71.

"The Devotional Poets of the Seventeenth Century: Donne, Herbert, Crashaw." *Listener* 3 (26 March 1930): 552–53.

"Donne in Our Time." *A Garland for John Donne,* ed. Theodore Spencer. Harvard University Press, 1931, pp. 1–19.

" 'A Dream within a Dream': T. S. Eliot on Edgar Allan Poe." *Listener* 29 (25 Feb. 1943): 243–44.

Essays Ancient and Modern. Faber and Faber, 1936.

"Ezra Pound." *Poetry* 68 (1946): 326–38.

For Lancelot Andrewes. Faber and Gwyer, 1928.

"From Poe to Valéry." *Hudson Review* 2 (autumn 1949): 327–42.

"The Frontiers of Criticism" (1956). *On Poetry and Poets.* Farrar, Straus and Cudahy, 1961, pp. 113–34.

"The Function of Criticism" (1923). *Selected Essays.* Harcourt, Brace & World, 1960, pp. 12–24.

"George Herbert." *Spectator* 5411 (12 March 1932): 360–61.

George Herbert. Longmans, Green, 1962.

"Goethe as the Sage" (1955). *On Poetry and Poets.* Farrar, Straus and Cudahy, 1961, pp. 240–64.

Homage to John Dryden. Hogarth Press, 1924.

"Individualists in Verse." *New English Weekly* 30 (14 Nov. 1946): 52.

"In Memoriam" (1936). *Selected Essays.* Harcourt, Brace & World, 1960, pp. 286–98.

"Inquiry into the Spirit and Language of Night." *Transition* 27 (April / May 1938): 236.

Introduction. G. Wilson Knight, *The Wheel of Fire.* Methuen, 1930, pp. xi–xix.

Introduction. *Literary Essays of Ezra Pound,* ed. T. S. Eliot. Faber and Faber, 1954, pp. ix–xv.

Introduction (1928). Ezra Pound, *Selected Poems,* ed. T. S. Eliot. Faber and Faber, 1948, pp. 7–21.

Introduction. Marianne Moore, *Selected Poems.* Macmillan, 1935, pp. vii–xiv.

Introduction. Paul Valéry, *The Art of Poetry,* trans. Denise Folliot. Vintage Books, 1958, pp. vii–xxiv.

"Isolated Superiority." *Dial* 84 (1928): 4–7.

"Israfel." *Nation and Athenaeum* 41 (1927): 219.

"An Italian Critic on Donne and Crashaw." *Times Literary Supplement* 1248 (17 Dec. 1925): 878.

"John Donne." *Nation and Athenaeum* 33 (1923): 331–32.

"John Dryden" (1921). *Selected Essays.* Harcourt, Brace & World, 1960, pp. 264–74.

"Johnson as Critic and Poet" (1944). *On Poetry and Poets.* Farrar, Straus and Cudahy, 1961, pp. 184–222.

"Johnson's *London* and *The Vanity of Human Wishes.*" *English Critical Essays: Twentieth Century,* ed. Phyllis M. Jones, 1933, pp. 301–10.

"Lancelot Andrewes" (1926). *Selected Essays.* Harcourt, Brace & World, 1960, pp. 299–319.

"Leçon de Valéry." *Quarterly Review of Literature* 3 (spring 1947): 212–14.

"Literature and the Modern World." *American Prefaces* 1 (Nov. 1935): 19–22.

"Marianne Moore." *Dial* 75 (1923): 594–97.

"The Metaphysical Poets" (1921). *Selected Essays.* Harcourt, Brace & World, 1960, pp. 241–50.

"Milton I" (1936). *On Poetry and Poets.* Farrar, Straus and Cudahy, 1961, pp. 156–64.

"Milton II" (1947). *On Poetry and Poets.* Farrar, Straus, and Cudahy, 1961, pp. 165–83.

"The Minor Metaphysicals: From Cowley to Dryden." *Listener* 3 (9 April 1930): 641–42.

"Mystic and Politician as Poet: Vaughan, Traherne, Marvell, Milton." *Listener* 3 (2 April 1930), 590–91.

"The Music of Poetry" (1942). *On Poetry and Poets.* Farrar, Straus and Cudahy, 1961, pp. 17–33.

"The Mysticism of Blake." *Nation and Athenaeum* 41 (1937): 779.

"*The Name and Nature of Poetry* by A. E. Housman." *Criterion* 13 (1933): 151–54.

"A Note on Poetry and Belief." *Enemy* 1 (Jan. 1927): 15–17.

"A Note on Richard Crashaw." *For Lancelot Andrewes.* Faber and Gwyer, 1928.

"A Note on Two Odes of Cowley." *Seventeenth-Century Studies Presented to Sir Herbert Grierson,* ed. John Dover Wilson. Clarendon Press, 1938, pp. 235–42.

"A Note on War Poetry." *London Calling,* ed. Storm Jameson. Harper & Brothers, 1942.

Notes Toward the Definition of Culture. Harcourt, Brace, 1949.

"Philip Massinger" (1920). *Selected Essays.* Harcourt, Brace & World, 1960, pp. 181–98.

"The Poems English Latin and Greek of Richard Crashaw." *Dial* 84 (1928): 246–50.

Poetry and Drama. Harvard University Press, 1951.

"The Poetry of W. B. Yeats." *Purpose* 12 (1940): 115–27.

Preface. *Anabasis: A Poem by St.-John Perse,* trans. T. S. Eliot. Harcourt, Brace, 1949, pp. 9–12.

"The Problem of the Shakespeare Sonnets." *Nation and Athenaeum* 40 (1927): 664, 666.

"Reflections on Contemporary Poetry I." *Egoist* 4, no. 8 (1917): 118–19.

"Reflections on Contemporary Poetry II." *Egoist* 4, no. 9 (1917): 113–34.

"Reflections on Contemporary Poetry III." *Egoist* 4, no. 10 (1917): 151.

"Reflections on Vers Libre." *New Statesman* 8 (1917): 518–19.

"Rhyme and Reason: The Poetry of John Donne." *Listener* 3 (19 March 1930): 502–3.

"Rudyard Kipling" (1941). *On Poetry and Poets.* Farrar, Straus and Cudahy, 1961, pp. 265–94.

"The Romantic Generation, If It Existed." *Athenaeum* 4655 (18 July 1919): 616–17.

The Sacred Wood: Essays on Poetry and Criticism. Methuen, 1928.

"Second Thoughts about Humanism" (1928). *Selected Essays.* Harcourt, Brace & World, 1960, pp. 429–438.

"Shakespeare and the Stoicism of Seneca" (1927). *Selected Essays.* Harcourt, Brace & World, 1960, pp. 107–20.

"The Silurist." *Dial* 83 (1927): 259–63.

"The Social Function of Poetry" (1945). *On Poetry and Poets.* Farrar, Straus and Cudahy, 1961, pp. 3–16.

"Swinburne as Poet" (1920). *Selected Essays.* Harcourt, Brace & World, 1960, pp. 281–85.

"Tennyson and Whitman." *Nation and Athenaeum* 41 (1927): 302.

"Thinking in Verse: A Survey of Early Seventeenth-Century Poetry." *Listener* 3 (12 March 1930): 441–43.

"The Three Voices of Poetry" (1953). *On Poetry and Poets.* Farrar, Straus and Cudahy, 1961, pp. 96–112.

The Use of Poetry and the Use of Criticism: Studies in the Relation of Criticism to Poetry in England. Harvard University Press, 1933.

"Verse Pleasant and Unpleasant." *Egoist* 5 (March 1918): 43–44.

"Virgil and the Christian World" (1951). *On Poetry and Poets.* Farrar, Straus and Cudahy, 1961, pp. 135–48.

"What Is a Classic?" (1944). *On Poetry and Poets.* Farrar, Straus and Cudahy, 1961, pp. 52–74.

"What Is Minor Poetry?" (1944). *On Poetry and Poets.* Farrar, Straus and Cudahy, 1961, pp. 34–51.

"Whitman and Tennyson." *Nation and Athenaeum* 40 (1926): 426.

"Yeats" (1940). *On Poetry and Poets.* Farrar, Straus and Cudahy, 1961, pp. 295–308.

OTHER AUTHORS

Abrams, M. H. *Natural Supernaturalism: Tradition and Revolution in Romantic Literature.* W. W. Norton, 1971.

Brooks, Cleanth. *The Hidden God: Studies in Hemingway, Faulkner, Yeats, Eliot, and Warren.* Yale University Press, 1963.

The Cloud of Unknowing. Trans. Clifton Walters. Penguin Books, 1961.

Gardner, Helen. *The Art of T. S. Eliot.* Cresset Press, 1949.

Hall, Donald. "The Art of Poetry I: T. S. Eliot: An Interview." *Paris Review* 11 (spring, summer, 1959): 63.

John of the Cross. *The Collected Works of St. John of the Cross,* trans. Kieren Kavanaugh, O. C. D., and Otilio Rodriguez, O. C. D. Institute of Carmelite Studies Publications, 1973.

Juliana of Norwich. *Revelations of Divine Love,* trans. Clifton Walters. Penguin Books, 1966.

Keats, John. *The Poems of John Keats,* ed. E. De Selincourt. Methuen, 1905.

Kirk, Russell. *Eliot and His Age: T. S. Eliot's Moral Imagination in the Twentieth Century.* Random House, 1971.

Matthiessen, F. O. *The Achievement of T. S. Eliot: An Essay on the Nature of Poetry,* 1935; 3rd ed., 1958, rpt. Oxford University Press, 1972.

Olson, Elder James, ed. *American Lyric Poems.* Appleton, 1964.

———. *Aristotle's Poetics and English Literature.* Chicago University Press, 1965.

———. "An Outline of Poetic Theory." *Critics and Criticism, Ancient and Modern,* ed. R. S. Crane. Chicago University Press, 1952, pp. 546–66.

Preston, Raymond. *Four Quarters Rehearsed.* Sheed and Ward, 1947.

Rootham, Cyril Bradley. *"On the Morning of Christ's Nativity" by John Milton, for 3 (or 2) soloists, chorus, semichorus and orchestra.* Stainer and Bell, 1928.

Tennyson, Alfred Lord. *The Poems of Tennyson,* ed. Christopher Ricks. Longman, 1969.

Unger, Leonard. "T. S. Eliot, 1888–1965. Viva la Poeta!" *Massachusetts Review* (spring–winter 1965): pp. 408–10.

Van Doren, Mark. "The Possible Importance of Poetry" (1951); rpt. in *The Happy Critic and Other Essays.* Hill & Wang, 1961, pp. 14–24.

Williams, R. Vaughan. *Epithalamion, a cantata for baritone solo, chorus, and small orchestra. Based on the masque "The Bridal Day." Words by E. Spenser.* Oxford University Press, 1957.

INDEX